Contents

Francis Ford Coppola, the wonder be

1 Hollywood Lullaby

It could be one of the golden stories that Hollywood portrayed so well in the past. All the ingredients are there.

It could be the story of an ugly duckling whose early years were marked by extreme solitude and a feverish desire for success and glory.

His childhood was a privileged period, the memory of which will be idealized with the passage of time. He will seek refuge in it, in its timeless memories, "over the rainbow," where adults cannot go. . . .

Francis Coppola was born on April 7, 1939, in Detroit, Michigan, where his parents, Carmine and Italia Coppola, had lived for two years.

His father, Carmine, was then the assistant conductor and arranger for "The Ford Sunday Evening Hour," a weekly radio concert, broadcast nationally and sponsored by the automobile magnate Henry Ford. And since Francis was born in the Henry Ford Hospital, his parents decided to include Ford in their son's name. He was named Francis after his maternal grandfather, Francesco Pennino, a famous Italian composer of the early twentieth century, whose fame was rekindled in the score of *The Godfather, Part II*. Italia Coppola regrets having Americanized her son's name because his personality is "so Italian."

"May Papa Be Successful"

Carmine Coppola, who is of Neopolitan ancestry, was born in New York, where he learned to play the flute at an early age. He attended the Juilliard School of Music, where he studied to be a composer and orchestra conductor. Soon after his marriage to Italia Pennino, he was named first flutist with the Radio City Music Hall Orchestra in New York City. At the beginning of World War II, Carmine was solo flutist under the direction of Arturo Toscanini in the NBC Symphony Orchestra, where he remained for ten years. During the 1950s, in search of success, Carmine Coppola turned to Broadway, where he was the conductor of several orchestras.

Francis has a brother, August, five years his elder, and a younger sister named Talia. He remembers "constant moving, within a warm, loving, and active environment, replete with upheavals, shouting, and passion." His father played an important role: "He was a man of great talent who was the focus of our lives. We were all concerned about what we felt was the tragedy of his career." Coppola remembers that the evening prayers recited before their mother always ended with "and may Papa be successful." "It was the main leitmotif of my family."

Carmine Coppola was an extremely ambitious man whose dream was to know glory as a composer and orchestra conductor. Music, omnipresent music, is one of Francis's earliest memories. As his career progressed, Coppola often turned to his father for the musical scores for his films.

The father-son relationship remains an ambiguous one, however, as confirmed by the following anecdote: At one point while the family was living in New York, Francis was working for Western Union. "For some unknown reason—I still don't know why—I sent my father a telegram hiring him to write the music for *Jet Star* and I signed the name of the music director for Paramount. My father was deliriously happy, screaming, 'That's it, I've succeeded, I've succeeded.' Finally, I had to admit what I had done and it broke his heart. It is a terrible story."

At the age of nine, he contracted polio and remained at home for a year. He occupied himself with a theater of puppets and hours upon hours of television. "I was lost in a fairy world," he recounts, adding: "The popular kids are playing outside, not lost in introspection. But the lonely ugly duckling is inside, sick and sad and thinking." Already he was worried about not being recognized and despairing at the idea of being an ordinary man. "The illness separated me from other children and taught me solitude."

In 1949, at the age of ten, he began making his first films using a 16-millimeter camera and a tape recorder. Most of these films were home movies or cartoons. "I starred in them and I even made some money with them as I would show them to the kids in the neighborhood." Using the same principle, he later wrote love letters for his college friends, charging one dollar per page.

Francis envied his older brother August, who was "better-looking and more intelligent." He saw himself as a kid who was "funny-looking, bad in school, and myopic," whereas August was "brighter and more mature than others his age." "He was my older brother, he took care of me and still did well in school. . . . He made me read a great deal, and thanks to him I discovered André Gide, Jean-Paul Sartre, and James Joyce. I was fourteen at the time."

Francis then attended a private school in Cornwall-on-Hudson, north of New York City. Furious when the words he had written for a class musical were changed without his consent, he transferred to a military school. Having shortly thereafter run away from this school, he finally obtained his high school diploma from Great Neck High School on Long Island.

"I was about eighteen when I became a disciple of Eisenstein." He read everything he could find on Eisenstein and saw every one of his films at the Museum of Modern Art. "I was dying to make a film. So, following his example, I studied the theater and worked very hard. I could build and light a set. I wanted to know everything, from every aspect, to have the same breadth of knowledge as Eisenstein did, for that was how he began."

Big Man on Campus

In the fall of 1956, he entered Hofstra College (now Hofstra University) where, during his first year, he was made editor of the theatrical and musical columns of the school literary publication, *World*.

He published a short story, "Candide, or Pessimism," which he signed François-Marie Arouet de Coppola! Its hero, Candide, lives in Great Neck with his master of thought, Doctor Grimes, who teaches him to live in "the worst of worlds." At the beginning, Candide goes along with him and therefore refuses the advances of his sister-in-law Cunégonde. After having traveled the world and suffered a great deal in his quest for fortune and glory, Candide, who is about to die of starvation, is cared for by a magnificent creature, a true goddess who is none other than Cunégonde, who has undergone plastic surgery. When Doctor Grimes speaks to him once again of the furies of hell, Candide dismisses him. As he is about to make love to Cunégonde, Candide cries out: "What a pile of shit I was taught when I was young." Because of its audacity and the precociousness of its themes, the story was a great success. Its form was good, its style alert, and its anti-intellectualism made it even more appealing.

Coppola wrote three more short stories during his first eighteen months at Hofstra: "The Garden of the Little Pink Princess," "The Battle for the Lions," which takes place during the Middle Ages, and "Del Vecchio," which appeared in the autumn 1957 issue of *World*.

Coppola remained in charge of the column until the winter of 1959, but he spent his energy elsewhere. From the very start of his academic career, he was involved in the drama department, where he met James Caan, who would eventually star in *The Rain People* and *The Godfather.*

Coppola worked on the production of *Hamlet* in 1958. He even played a few parts in *Once in a Lifetime, Best Foot Forward,* and *As You Like It.* The following year, he was in charge of the lighting for *Hamlet, Light Up the Sky,* and *Of Thee I Sing,* a musical comedy by Gershwin that marked his last appearance on the stage. He was involved in the staging of *Picnic,* and won the Dan H. Laurence Award for his production of Eugene O'Neill's

The Rope, which was, according to the university's dean, "the best ever done by a student."

He also adapted *Inertia* from a story by H. G. Wells, "The Man Who Could Work Miracles." He co-directed and wrote both the dialogue and musical score for this project, which was very successful and encouraged Coppola in his quest for fame. He was, by then, the "big man on campus," a very important fact for him: he was "an average student who nevertheless became the central figure of the drama department. It was also the first time I had the sole responsibility for my own production. And I commanded as much power here as I might on the outside."

During his last year, he directed stagings of *A Streetcar Named Desire* and a musical comedy, *A Delicate Touch,* both of which were very well received.

UCLA

During this period he also founded the Cinema Workshop, and had even sold his car in order to buy a 16-millimeter camera to achieve his most cherished wish: to make a film. He imagined a story about a mother who takes her two children to the country for the afternoon. After showing them the beautiful countryside, she falls asleep, and, when she wakes, the children are gone. "The idea," says Coppola, "was to show that what had been so beautiful before, had suddenly become horrible, menacing, and dangerous because of the disappearance of the children. I wanted to experiment with this duality, but I only filmed one part of it and never finished the project. I had no technical experience then."

To improve these techniques, Coppola enrolled at UCLA in 1960, but was soon disenchanted by the school, where he felt lonely. "There was none of the camaraderie I had imagined while I was in college." He had expected it to be the ideal place "where everyone would be working together,

making films and drinking wine, all in the company of beautiful women."

Coppola's disillusionment was the result not only of his age but of his environment, of students who were, in fact, directly his opposite. "All they knew," he commented bitterly, "was how to criticize the lazy ways of Hollywood film producers, implying that only they could be capable of directing great films." As for the teaching, his opinion was no better: "We wanted to learn how to make a film. That was all we cared about. And as our only answer, we were entitled to a conference with Stanley Kramer, who had come

to talk about the reasons for his success." What's more, "we were given minuscule amounts of 8-millimeter film, we were put in a field and told to bring back a film. . . . Little by little, we learned to work with sound, but never to synchronize. We occasionally had access to 16-millimeter and finally to the Moviola. At the end of the year, the professor would choose two students who, with whatever money was available, were to make two films that would be representative of the students' project."

Coppola jumped at the first opportunity to perfect his technique and di-

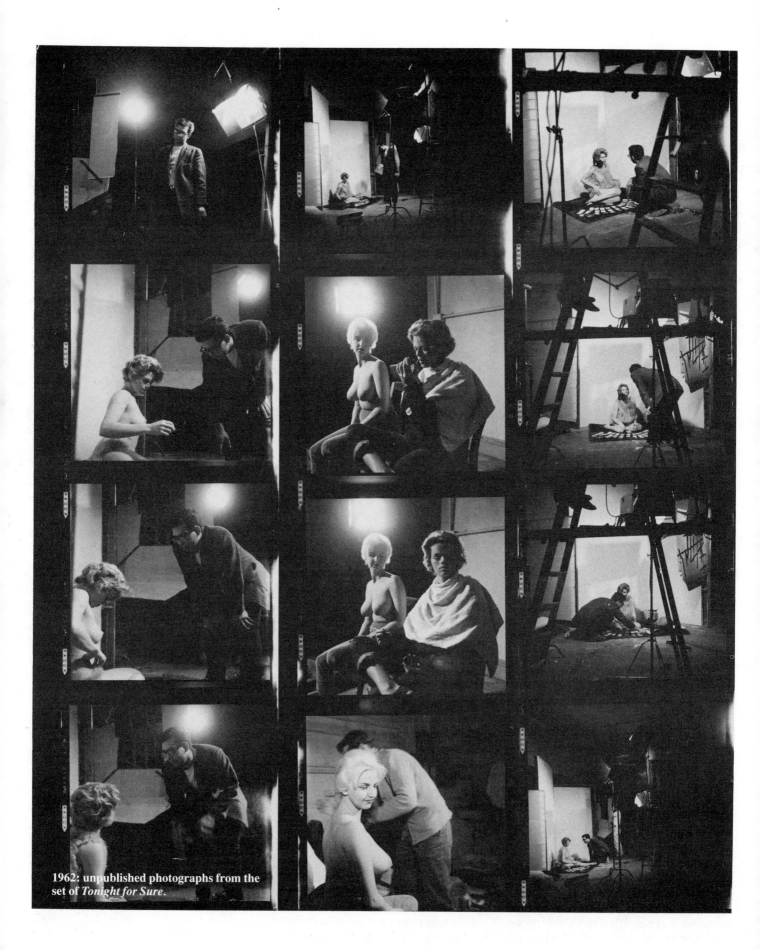

1962: unpublished photographs from the set of *Tonight for Sure*.

rected three "nudie films"! The first was entitled *The Peeper.* "It was a rather clever idea," says Coppola, "about a man who discovers quite by chance that pin-up girls are being photographed in the next apartment. The entire film traces this man's efforts to see what is going on in the neighboring apartment. But he never succeeds. At one point, using a powerful telescope, he manages to catch a glimpse of a girl's belly button! Similarly, all his other attempts end in failure."

The second film, *Tonight for Sure,* was produced for a "company that had previously made a 'western nudie' with a cowboy who, having been hit on the head, saw all his cows as naked women! It was amazing," remembers Coppola.

Finally, another film company hired him for several days long enough to "add five three-minute sequences, in color, to a stupid German film that had been shot in black and white," entitled *The Belt Girl and the Playboy.* Coppola does not apologize for any of these as "it was the only way for me to work with a camera and make a film." At UCLA, he was discovered by Dorothy Arzner, a professor at the college and one of the few women directors at RKO, who had worked with stars such as Joan Crawford, Clara Bow, Fredric March, Rosalind Russell, and Katharine Hepburn. Coppola was grateful for the help she brought him. But it was a small posted notice, informing the students that Roger Corman was looking for an assistant, that really put Coppola on the road toward his eventual success.

The Corman Years

Roger Corman's biography resembles that of Frank Capra. Like Capra, Corman holds an engineering degree; like him, he served in the army, then took odd jobs waiting for the right opportunity: he collected unemployment benefits, worked for a time at a television station, then was a reader for a literary agent. "While I was there, I read all kinds of terrible scripts that were in-

tended for B movies," Corman remembers. "I knew that I could do, if not better, as least as well." In just a few nights he wrote his first screenplay, *Highway Dragnet,* which he sold to Allied Artists for four thousand dollars.

With this money, and some more borrowed from his family, Corman wrote a second screenplay, *The Monster from the Ocean Floor.* Although the story took place in Mexico, it was filmed in Malibu, in the space of six days and at the cost of $12,000! The film earned $100,000. . . . Corman then founded Roger Corman Productions. One of the first directors to employ Jack Nicholson, he knew how to attract and recognize future talents, such as Robert De Niro, Peter Fonda, Ellen Burstyn, Diane Ladd, Martin Scorsese, Haskell Wexler, Robert Towne (the future screenwriter for *Shampoo*), and Coppola.

First Appearance in the Credits

"After having been caught in the trap of the porn market, I felt as if I were climbing the ranks of the cinema industry" says Coppola. "I was prepared to do anything in order to direct more films, and for me, the best opportunity was this open field represented by the commercial cinema."

His UCLA friends regarded his decision as a form of treason; they would never stoop to such a contemptible form of cinema. Coppola earned his first salary—"two hundred and fifty dollars for six months of work"—for the English dubbing of a Russian science-fiction film, *Battle Beyond the Sun*! The fact that he did not know a single word of Russian did not concern Coppola: "In the end, the new version of the film had nothing in common with the original one." Corman turned the Russian cosmonauts into monsters and added a few erotic scenes to enliven the film.

Coppola was credited as a screenwriter for the first time while working for Corman. "I tried to impress Roger

every way I could. I purposely worked nights, so that he would find me the next morning, bleary-eyed, working with the Moviola." Coppola soon became Corman's right-hand man. When Corman needed a sound engineer for *The Young Racers.* Coppola promptly offered his services. He quickly read through *The Perfectone Sound Recorder* before leaving for Europe, where he served as the film's sound man, apparently to the great satisfaction of Corman. But his name is overlooked in the film's credits.

A short time later, he served his master once again. Having completed the filming of *The Raven* earlier than anticipated, Corman still had use of the set for two more days. He informed Coppola that Boris Karloff was prepared to work two additional days while the set was still available. "I had to wrack my brain to make the best use of these two days and end up with something credible," laughs Coppola. They began shooting without a script . . . purposely. "At one point, a young soldier from Napoleon's army, played by Jack Nicholson, arrived at the castle to meet Karloff who, for some unknown reason, ordered Nicholson to leave immediately. What could he do? He killed Nicholson's horse. And I had to invent a logical explanation for Karloff's act."

The film was a disaster, but Corman, Nicholson, and Coppola completed it nonetheless, and Coppola thus earned the credit of assistant producer. In order to avoid an impending lawsuit brought by Karloff, Corman eventually asked Peter Bogdanovich to incorporate some of the cuts from *The Terror* (the above-mentioned film) in Bogdanovich's first film, *Targets.*

Dementia 13

Possibly because Coppola knew how to handle Corman, but also because Corman recognized the qualities of his young protégé, Corman gave Coppola the opportunity to direct his own film. Coppola knew that Corman wished to use his crew to make another film right after completing *The Young Racers*. He reacted quickly and came up with a story he could direct.

"I sold the film to Roger based on one single scene," explains Coppola. "It is night. We are in Dublin. A woman emerges from a castle, carrying a bag. She stops and takes out five dolls from the bag and attaches them by the neck to a weight. Then, she gets undressed and plunges into the lake. The dolls rise to the surface of the water and float there. The woman begins turning around and finds the body of a seven-year-old girl with long hair floating about her. The woman runs out of the water, screaming, before being hacked to death with an ax."

"Roger said to me: do it," recounts Coppola, who adds: "I did not have the slightest idea of what this woman was doing." Corman supplied twenty thousand dollars and Coppola wrote the script in three days. He then met an English producer by the name of Raymond Stross, who advanced him an additional twenty thousand dollars for the rights to distribute the film in Great Britain. Corman, who was displeased, threatened to pull out, but Coppola had already transferred the money into another bank account. Needled by Corman, Coppola knew exactly what he had to do: "The film would have to be a commercial success, in the style of *Psycho.*"

The shoot began, and each day Coppola would receive a cable from Corman demanding more sex and violence. But it was fun. Coppola invited his California friends to participate in his adventure. "We were young and we were making a film," he remembers with nostalgia, adding, "It was the only film I really enjoyed making." Among the people who joined Coppola on the set in 1962 was Eleonor Neil, featured in the credits as the set designer.

Once *Dementia 13* was completed, Coppola canceled an engagement in Yugoslavia and returned to the United States to marry Eleonor. He realized that *Dementia 13* was full of promise. "It was more than an accumulation of clichés. Visually, the film is one of my best accomplishments. I had composed each shot in detail. Today, such work is no longer feasible, it takes too long."

The story of *Dementia 13* focuses on John Holoran and his wife Louise. While walking along the lake on the grounds of John's estate, the couple argue because Louise can only benefit from Lady Holoran's will if John, who has a weak heart, remains alive. Upset by the discussion, John suffers a heart attack and dies. Louise pushes his body into the lake and tells the family—Lady Holoran and her two other sons, Richard and Billy—that he has gone to New York. Louise decides to drive Lady Holoran mad (Lady Holoran is still in mourning for her daughter Kathleen). But as she is conjuring up a plan, Louise is savagely murdered with an ax near the lake (this is the greatly revised scene originally described to Corman).

Before Louise's death, Kane, Richard's fiancée, had tried in vain to convince him to leave the estate. She sympathizes with Billy, who has suffered from terrible nightmares ever since the death of his sister.

Simon, an old friend of the family, is also killed with an ax during a hunt. Lady Holoran suddenly comes across her daughter's doll house, which has been destroyed by an ax. The family physician orders that the lake be drained and plans to unmask the murderer during Richard and Kane's wedding. The plan works and Billy is revealed as being the killer. But Billy is then killed while trying to murder Kane.

The film clearly suffers from several shortcomings, the least of which are the missing pieces in the script, which made the film difficult to follow. For example, when the lake has been drained, an inscribed stone made in memory of Kathleen turns up, but not John's body! And nothing about Billy's behavior (except perhaps his nightmares) could lead one to assume he was the murderer. Patrick Magee (as the physician) makes too much of it, alas! Nevertheless, the other actors are quite convincing.

One must point out the effectiveness of the fantastic and disquieting credit sequence, wherein John's body is seen swinging back and forth in front of the camera, as in a macabre water ballet. One can already recognize the "Coppolian" mastery of the camera. The heavy and brooding atmosphere captures our imagination and lends credibility to certain unfathomable events. All in all, it was an encouraging first production of which Coppola could be proud.

Released in New York in 1963, *Dementia 13* attracted the attention of only a few critics. Of those who saw the film, Howard Thompson of *The New York Times* was the only one to review it, and he gave a severe and in-depth commentary: "Under the dismal direction of Francis Coppola, who also wrote the screenplay, what is a rather plausible story is drowned in blood." But Coppola was unruffled; in record time, he had accomplished his life's goal and had earned his first stripes. His unusual early experiences had offered him a global view of his chosen profession as he had been, at different times, an editor, a sound engineer, a screenplay writer, and, finally, a director.

In 1962, he was awarded the Samuel Goldwyn award for his screenplay of *Pilma Pilma,* an honor which afforded him entry into Seven Arts, which purchased the film rights for the script, but chose not to produce it. Upon his return from Ireland, Coppola was hired by Seven Arts as a screenwriter. His UCLA classmates would never forgive him his rapid success. "The day I got my first job as a screenwriter," he remembers, "they had put up a sign about me that read: 'Sold.' For, in their eyes, I had sold out. They hated me because I was making money and wasn't ashamed of it."

Five Hundred Dollars a Week

Those who accused Coppola of siding with the cinema's Establishment were

The warrior at rest.

undoubtedly vexed to learn that Seven Arts turned to him for the screenplay adaptation of Carson McCullers's novel *Reflections in a Golden Eye.* "The company had bought the rights but did not know what to do with it. They were about to drop the option because so much money had been invested in the project. The only solution was to find someone who could make the film for very little money."

Impressed by Coppola's work, Seven Arts offered him a three-year contract as a screenwriter, at a salary of five hundred dollars a week. His contributions to the script of *Reflections in a Golden Eye,* as to other screenplays he would eventually work on, were considerable, and yet his name did not appear in the credits of John Huston's film.

Coppola moved right on to the production of *This Property Is Condemned,* based on a one-act play by Tennessee Williams, to be directed by Sidney Pollack. This time, he worked with Edith Sommer. Together, they made some important changes in Tennessee Williams's text. In the play, Willie is a young girl who walks along the railroad tracks and meets a young man to whom she speaks of her missing sister, Alva.

The film, however focuses more on Alva (Natalie Wood), who falls in love with Owen Legate (Robert Redford, in one of his earliest parts). Alva's mother, Hazel (Kate Reid), tries to convince Owen that Alva is not the girl for him, for she has other plans for Alva: she wants her to marry someone else. Once Owen is gone, Alva takes her revenge by marrying her mother's lover. She leaves him immediately and joins Owen in New Orleans. Her mother, in turn, gets even by informing Owen of Alva's marriage. Caught in a trap, Alva loses her mind and eventually dies of tuberculosis.

The critics were merciless, in spite of the stars' performances. The screenplay writers were even accused of having built "a totally incredible story."

In his defense, Coppola answered that a screenplay is never definitive, it is only the rough draft of a film. "That becomes obvious as soon as you try to direct the screenplay you have written."

In defense of authors in general, he went on to say: "Most of those who share in the credits of a film have never worked together in Hollywood before. For one is immediately replaced by another, then another. . . . It is like leaving the house of a girl with whom you have lived, while her new boyfriend is moving in. It's terrible."

Coppola adds: "The position of the screenwriter is an absurd, ridiculous one. He earns a great deal of money but has no say whatsoever about the film, unless he is one of the more famous screenwriters. This is particularly true for young authors."

After one year at Seven Arts, Coppola's salary was raised to $1,000 a week. He spent no money at the time and thus saved $20,000, with which he could do very little. "I was very frustrated," he says. "I could have bought myself a Ferrari or a sailboat, but I could not make a film." He decided to invest all of his money in the stock market, buying shares of Scopitone, manufacturer of a "jukebox" for short films, hoping to see his initial investment grow to over $100,000. But Coppola lost everything and it was time to start all over again.

Is Paris Burning?

Seven Arts offered Coppola the opportunity to stay in Paris during the filming of *Is Paris Burning?,* to be directed by René Clément. "What that meant," he says, "was that I waited for Anthony Veiller to drop his pen, so that I could take over."

The situation was rendered all the more uncomfortable by the fact that Veiller thought of Coppola as his assistant. "He would ask me to come to his hotel and would say, 'I would like you to rewrite this scene, and then that one.' I knew he was dying and could not say anything. For five weeks, I would go to him every morning and he would mock my work. I was very unhappy. Finally, he died, and I went to see the producer to tell him that I was leaving."

But Coppola had to wait until the arrival of Gore Vidal, who was to complete the unfinished screenplay. The atmosphere was detestable, for René Clément was groveling at the feet of the producer, Paul Graetz, simply because he did not speak a work of English. "The problem was the following: The French government would permit us to film in the streets of Paris as long as the word 'communist' was never mentioned in the film's script," recounts Coppola. In fact, the producers were afraid of making a film that would displease de Gaulle.

At the same time, Gore Vidal and Coppola learned that three other French screenwriters, Claude Brulé, Jean Aurenche, and Pierre Bost, were writing three other parallel screenplays. The final version of this screenplay was a blend of the four scripts, but only Gore Vidal and Francis Coppola's names were listed in the credits, thanks to the screenwriters' union in the United States.

Is Paris Burning? takes place in 1944, at the time when the members of the Resistance have regained control of the capital and have learned that the Allies had decided to bypass Paris. The Resistance leaders convince the Allies nevertheless to send a few units to Paris. During this time, General von Choltitz, who had orders from Hitler to burn Paris, stalls, not wishing to be remembered, in the eyes of history, as the one who destroyed the French capital. The outcome is well known: He disobeys, leaving the Americans and the French the opportunity to liberate Paris.

The film was adapted from the famous book written by Dominique Lapierre and Larry Collins. When the film was released, it was received coolly. *Newsweek,* in its terse review, commented that "the incompetence, the laziness or the haste of the production caused the screenwriters, Gore Vidal and Francis Coppola, to bulldozer the complexities of history." The reviewers for *Time* magazine said that: *"Is Paris Burning?* is assuredly the most confused film on the war. For history is being told from sixty different viewpoints at the same time." The critics were rough, but Coppola had other more pressing worries.

He still owed ten thousand dollars to the bank, and had a wife and two children to support. There was more: during the filming of *Is Paris Burning?* he had spent his free time writing an original script which would become *You're a Big Boy Now.* And Seven Arts, claiming that this work had been done on their time, while he was on their salary, wanted to take over all rights to this project.

The deluge of *Apocalypse Now.*

Elizabeth Hartman seduces Peter Kastner in *You're a Big Boy Now*. (Warner-Columbia Films)

2 Sweet Bird of Youth

You're a Big Boy Now

After his considerable financial losses, Coppola needed a miracle. In the way that reality is often more fantastic than fiction, even cinematic fiction, providence appeared in the form of 20th Century–Fox. The major film company offered Coppola fifty thousand dollars to write a screenplay about the life of General Patton. This was not the first request for a screen adaptation of the subject. The final version, the one directed by Franklin J. Schaffner and starring the inimitable George C. Scott, was written by Coppola.

Coppola's reward for his work on this Hollywood superproduction came in 1970, when he won a well-deserved Oscar. In 1966, though, the project relieved Coppola of his temporary financial problems. This race against the dollar has always been a part of his career.

With the security of the fifty thousand dollars, Coppola turned to a project that he had been contemplating for a long time, and which became *You're a Big Boy Now*. This production was the result of an initial confrontation between, and the eventual combination of, a book (from which he took the title) and an idea of Coppola's. He had been puzzled for a long time by the strange habit—albeit a functional one—used by the young people working in the New York Public Library, who maintained the library stacks while wearing roller skates. Coppola had also wanted to portray the life of a teenager living in "the Big Apple."

Fifty-Fifty

He had to use great caution to protect his rights to the script, as his contract with Seven Arts stated that all screenplays were the property of the studio. But Seven Arts did not yet know the sly ways of the bearded man from Detroit. Coppola had discovered David Benedictus's novel, *You're a Big Boy Now,* and promptly bought its screen rights: he agreed to pay one thousand dollars for the option and ten thousand dollars upon the project's completion. The story concerns a nineteen-year-old man who works in a shoe store in London. "But there were so many similarities between this book and my own screenplay," says Coppola, "that it seemed as if we had both written the same story."

Seven Arts soon realized what was going on and demanded the rights to *You're a Big Boy Now.* Coppola answered: "I have the rights to the book from which the screenplay is taken. Therefore, I own one half and you the other. So let's do it together." After one year of negotiations with Phil Feldman, the producer, the final authorization was granted.

By the time the deliberations were concluded, Coppola wondered whether he even wanted to make this film. He decided in favor of it, but only after countless discussions, particularly those concerning the film's distribution rights.

Coppola could not get a box-office star to play the main part in *You're a Big Boy Now.* He then decided to select his actors in such a way that "each one of them alone would not represent an entity; but together, as a group, they had star quality." Without knowing them personally, he called Julie Harris, Geraldine Page, and Rip Torn. He also hired Elizabeth Hartman, Michael Dunn, Peter Kastner, and an actress unknown at the time, Karen Black.

This list reassured Seven Arts in its hopes of minimizing its financial risks and of being able to sell the film to television for a sum close to that of the production's cost. Once again, though, the budget got out of hand: it was initially supposed to be $250,000, but soon increased to nearly $1 million.

To further entice the actors, the young director offered them the chance to play roles that were the opposite of those they usually portrayed.

Two Scripts for One Film

You're a Big Boy Now gave Coppola the opportunity to experiment with a personal type of direction. He wrote two screenplays: "The first one was very visual, and described the point of the film. The second was oriented more toward dialogue than description."

The actors worked mainly with the second screenplay. They rehearsed in a small theater, without any stage sets or props. After filming rough cuts on television cameras, Coppola then gave his actors the second screenplay, destined for the actual filming.

Despite this meticulous preparation, Coppola felt ill at ease when the moment came to start the actual filming. "I did not enjoy making that film," he confides. "I was scared. My other staging experiences, both in the theater and in films, had brought me great pleasure. But this time, I was in New York. I was working with a real team of union technicians and I had a fixed and strictly limited shooting schedule."

The pressure mounted. "The first day on the set, you could feel the panic. I was pacing back and forth across a stage I had never seen before. Nine actors and a crew of forty technicians waited for me to tell them what to do. The cameraman asked me where to position the first camera. I had to tell him that I did not know. . . . Then, all of a sudden, I heard myself say: okay let's go. And forty-nine people were looking at me, waiting to see if I knew what I was talking about. I was becoming increasingly nervous, truly desperate, and finally had to ask them all to take a half an hour so that I could collect myself."

In spite of his earlier experience with *Dementia 13,* Coppola discovered how difficult it was to adapt the shot to the action. The relatively simple concept of filming two people speaking to each other—straight shot/reverse angle shot—became quite a complex task when the scene took place indoors and involved nine characters! Increasingly pressured, Coppola decided against filming the scenes in sequence. He felt that if he shot enough material, he could eventually edit the rushes correctly. When the shoot was over, he remained in New York with his editor, Aram Avakian. John Sebas-

tian (who would eventually appear in *Woodstock*) composed the musical score for the film. *Darling Be Home Soon*, one of his songs, was performed by his group, The Lovin' Spoonful.

With the help of the mayor, *You're a Big Boy Now* was granted a special authorization to film inside the New York Public Library. It was the first time that the famous library was ever seen on film.

Candide in New York

As he did in his short story "Candide, or Pessimism," Coppola chose the subject of a naïve nineteen-year-old for his film *You're a Big Boy Now*. Bernard Chanticleer (Peter Kastner) works as a clerk in the New York Public Library, where he moves about on roller skates.

Bernard's father (Rip Torn), a rare-books librarian within the same institution, feels that the time has come for his son to become a man. Bernard moves out of his home and into the rooming house of Miss Thing, who keeps an aggressive rooster in memory of her late brother.

Amy (Karen Black), a charming co-worker of Bernard's, likes him very much. She invites him to a discotheque in Greenwich Village. But when they are there, Bernard sees a young woman (Elizabeth Hartman) he has already noticed in the library. And from this moment on, he thinks only of her.

Amy, not willing to accept defeat, insists that Bernard invite her to his room. The initiative is spoiled by Miss Thing's rooster, which has a singular aversion toward women and attacks Amy. In the ensuing struggle, Bernard knocks Miss Thing down the stairs and she breaks her arm.

Bernard takes his family to see a play in which Barbara (Elizabeth Hartman) has a part. Convinced of his love, he writes her an impassioned letter.

Barbara receives the letter while she is dictating her memoirs to Richard, her confidant (and a dwarf). She tells

him that she has hated men ever since she was raped by a debauched albino hypnotist. She took her revenge by taking his wooden leg. She sees Bernard as an ideal victim, and lures him to her apartment with the sole intention of toying with him.

Bernard is eventually called to a "family meeting" which takes place in the library, to account for his transgressions. He flees, taking with him a rare and prized edition of a Gutenberg Bible.

A mad pursuit follows, resulting in Bernard's incarceration. Amy, who still loves him, comes to his rescue. This time, the moment has come for Bernard to "grow up."

The Knack or Not The Knack?

You're a Big Boy Now was presented at the 1967 Cannes Film Festival as the only American selection. It received mixed reviews.

Certain critics accused Coppola of having been over-influenced by Richard Lester's film *The Knack*.

Coppola answers: "It so happens that I wrote *You're a Big Boy Now* before Dick Lester's *The Knack* was even released. And yet everyone claims my film was a copy. If anything, I was influenced by *A Hard Day's Night*. But everything was there before I saw the film. . . . One of the difficulties of the film industry is that you are always forced to do things three years later."

Disillusioned but undefeated, Coppola expressed great admiration for the European cinema, especially the French cinema. It would not be incorrect to say that he, like many others, was influenced by the New Wave.

Some felt that *Big Boy* should have taken place in the London of the sixties. But Coppola's stroke of genius was precisely that he was able to transfer this universal subject, youth's search for answers, to New York.

Big Boy is a quest for identity, a rite of passage between adolescence and maturity. Bernard is seen coming out

of his shell with humor and tenderness. But in this kindly description, Coppola gives a far less indulgent one of a society—American or other—that stifles spontaneity, instinct, and the natural discovery of life beyond adolescence, a civilization that wishes to deprive the individual of the freedom of taking his time.

Big Boy was not a total success, but was an excellent exercise for a rookie of the Seventh Art named Coppola . . .

Finian's Rainbow

Coppola submitted *You're a Big Boy Now* as his thesis to complete his MFA degree requirements for UCLA. He then rented an office and began to write a new screenplay, the first pages of which eventually became *The Conversation*.

One day, Coppola's phone rang: "It was a guy asking me if I knew anyone who could direct *Finian's Rainbow*. I thought about it, gave him a few suggestions, and hung up. The following day, the man called me back and said: 'What about you?' "

Although Coppola had sworn to himself that he would not re-enter the world of the major film studios until he was prepared to fight them at their level, he accepted the offer. Many reasons influenced his decision, one of

Bernard is shy. (Warner-Columbia Films)

Elizabeth Hartman, the solitary dancer in
Big Boy. (Warner-Columbia Films)

Fred Astaire, the incorrigible dreamer of *Finian's Rainbow*. (Warner-Columbia Films)

which involved his father. As Carmine Coppola had already worked on several musicals, Francis thought that this project might please his father.

In 1947, *Finian's Rainbow* had been quite successful. It was, in Coppola's words, "a marvelous show of yesteryear that exuded warmth. I felt that if I could direct it well, if I could get the right equilibrium, I could give it a timeless dimension. . . . I've always been fond of musicals."

If the Vision Is Right

But Coppola's initial optimism soon turned sour. Rereading the play, he realized that the script was inadequate: the plot was ridiculous and the ideas, which in the 1940s had been liberal, were completely outdated by 1968. He then set about rewriting certain parts of the story (even though he would not receive any credit for his work). The rehearsals began, followed by the first days of shooting.

The heads of Warner Bros.–Seven Arts wanted the film's production to be swift and on schedule. Unfortunately, the insufficient time schedule resulted in several instances of poor synchronization. Coppola would eventually regret overlooking such details. Within the time given him, he tried to "squeeze out the essence of each scene." "I always believed that a director stages his film before even shooting the first frame. If his vision is correct, everything else will fall into place. Time would heal some of *Finian's Rainbow*'s major problems. But I am convinced that if the audience does not appreciate a film, it is because the vision was wrong."

In spite of the general optimism, the production problems began to multiply. Coppola had only three and a half weeks for rehearsals followed by twelve weeks of shooting. The schedule was too tight to allow him to do all that he had intended. He admitted that he was forced to fake certain shots, because he had only eight days of outdoor shooting. The rest of the time was spent in the studio. Under the circumstances, the difficulties he encountered in giving the film a natural look were understandable. During the final editing, the outdoor shots were carefully interspersed to give the illusion of reality. The rest was "faked," as they say in Hollywood. . . .

There were also problems in the choreography. "I had wanted personally to create the musical numbers. I used my inspiration. For example, for the 'Grandish' number, I thought I would show Petula Clark hanging white bedsheets on a hilltop." Coppola soon realized that the assigned choreographer—hired at the insistence of Fred Astaire—was "a disaster." He was fired halfway through the film's production and Coppola was forced to resort to more tricks: he used telephoto lenses and elaborate stage sets to mask the nearly absent choreography.

Copolla was uncomfortable with the way some of the actors approached their roles. For example, about Don Francks: "He never really improved as an actor. . . ." As for Tommy Steele, the director asserted, "I think I could have done better with him. While we were in rehearsals, Tommy was doing his thing. And I told him that I felt we were headed in the wrong direction. Everyone loved him and thought he was terrific. But I felt that Og, the elf, should have been played in a more coy, timid, and disoriented fashion. When I first started working on this film, I had wanted Donal Donnelly to play that part. I wanted an introverted elf, who would start speaking in a quiet voice and would suddenly become a human being."

"At my insistence, Tommy began to follow my instructions during rehearsals. And he was good. But actors are funny people. They rely on certain support systems, and they are hard pressed to relinquish them when they feel a little unsteady. As the shoot progressed, Tommy began slipping back to his original character. . . ." But Coppola only noticed this during the editing of the film.

Coppola's greatest handicap during the filming of *Finian's Rainbow* was probably the fact that he was, for the first time, working for a major film company. The tremendous responsibility of a multimillion-dollar project weighed heavily on his shoulders. He began to question the direction the project was taking as well as the problems only he saw as potentially serious.

Coppola later said: "I worked according to a methodology that I did not understand very well and over which I had no control. Whenever I would express a doubt about the way things were being handled, everyone around me said, 'It's going to be great!' Not one negative word was uttered during the entire production."

When the critics panned the film, Coppola remembered bitterly the exaggerated praises he had heard throughout the filming. He declared that he would never again work with people who were not capable of saying: "We're making a mistake."

Coppola had no control over the way *Finian's Rainbow* was presented to the public. It was featured in the larger movie theaters, but with only two shows per day. Also the tickets were higher priced than the usual, something that remains inexplicable as this musical comedy's budget was far lower than those of other films of the time. *Funny Girl* and *Star* cost nearly ten million dollars to produce, whereas *Finian's Rainbow*'s budget was only three and a half million dollars. But what was truly incomprehensible to Coppola was Warner Bros.' decision to blow up the film to 70-mm, turning it into a real "road show." By doing so, "they cut Fred Astaire's feet while he was dancing! No one had taken the trouble to check the top and bottom of the frame," says Coppola, with a touch of irony.

Too Weak an Intrigue

Finian McLonergan (Fred Astaire), accompanied by his daughter Sharon (Petula Clark), arrives in Fort Knox, Missitucky, from his native Ireland. His intention is to turn this area into the valley of happiness. He is sure of his success, thanks to his magical golden bowl taken from an Irish elf named Og. Finian arrives just in time to save Woody (Don Francks), a brave man, from being ruined by an evil senator (Keenan Wynn) who wants to dispossess Woody of his property. Woody and Sharon fall in love at first sight.

Problems arise for Woody when he learns from some geologists that there is gold under his land. By now, Senator Rawkins's greed is even stronger than before. Sharon, who is something of a witch, puts a curse on Rawkins by turning him into a black man. Rawkins goes into hiding and Sharon is charged with his kidnapping. Then everything goes wrong: Og, the elf, has followed Finian to force him to return the golden bowl that makes him immortal. But the bowl has vanished!

Meanwhile, Sharon has been accused of sorcery. Suddenly, everything works out for the best: Og falls in love with Woody's sister and renounces his immortality; Rawkins regains his original skin; Sharon is not burned at the stake, and she marries Woody. The tobacco fields become incredibly fertile, and the story ends with dancing and songs, while the incorrigible Finian leaves Missitucky to follow other dreams.

Years later, Coppola still questions some of his strategic decisions concerning the film's production: "I thought that to make a film of *Finian's Rainbow,* I would not need to rewrite and update it. I think I was wrong. I think that the timing was wrong for such a film." One cannot deny the weakness of the plot and its inability to hold the interest of the audience in the late sixties, at a time when so many events were changing the social structure of society, especially in the United States.

The timing of a film's release plays a very important role in its reception by the public. But the real problem was *Finian's Rainbow*'s fantasy elements, which worked better on the stage than on film, for on the big screen each

strange detail took on enormous proportions. Whereas theater audiences readily accept unrealistic situations, filmgoers require a more structured framework within which they can see the evolution of the plot. The main error in *Finian's Rainbow*'s production was to have tried to blend two incompatible genres.

Luckily for Coppola, this film did have some good points. Its main qualities were in its music track, with, in particular, the success of certain numbers such as "Look to the Rainbow," "Something Sort of Grandish," "How Are Things in Glocca Morra?" and "Old Devil Moon." Coppola did succeed in recapturing the warm feeling of the postwar musical comedies.

What's more, Petula Clark was a pleasure to listen to and to watch, although she sometimes seemed encumbered by the presence of Don Francks. Keenan Wynn was perfect, as usual, in his rendition of the bigoted and greedy senator. The main casting error concerned the leading role. Although Fred Astaire can brilliantly portray an elegant, sophisticated, and classy man, he did not fit the part of the bizarre and whimsical Finian. He actually seemed bored with the part, which in turn affected the rest of the film.

Coppola was somewhat inexperienced as a director then. He was still lacking what is, today, his indisputable talent (a talent which cannot be copied): a visionary power that encompasses in one sweep the totality of a film.

Coppola-Lucas: The Clash of the Stars

It was during the filming of *Finian's Rainbow* that Francis Ford Coppola met the young George Lucas. Lucas, at the time a recent graduate of the University of Southern California, had won a fellowship sponsored by Warner Bros. It gave him the opportunity to spend six months observing—

first-hand—the activities of a film studio. He was free to choose whatever area in which he wished to concentrate, and he chose animation. But, as a result of the economic crisis suffered by Hollywood during the 1960s, that particular department had been shut down. The only film currently in production in the famous Burbank studios was *Finian's Rainbow.* Its young bearded director was by then a legend to all the students of the cinema.

George Lucas: "Francis directed his first film while he was a student at UCLA and now, by God, he was doing a full-length feature film. That created shock waves in the world of the cinema because no one else had done that. It was a great accomplishment." Lucas's skinny silhouette became a fixture on the set. After two days, Coppola asked him who he was. Lucas answered him and expressed his desire to work with Coppola. "It was the beginning of a conversation and of a friendship," says Coppola.

Lucas was hired as Coppola's administrative assistant at a salary of three thousand dollars for six months' work. But after two weeks, Lucas had had enough. Coppola screamed: "What do you mean you are leaving? Am I not entertaining enough for you? Have you already learned everything you need to know by watching me direct?"

Lucas told him of a project concerning the film *THX 1138.* Coppola warned him of the dangers facing a young man when dealing with a large studio. He offered Lucas a permanent job, working on *Finian's Rainbow* as well as on his next planned project, *The Rain People,* and promised to help him with the screenplay of *THX 1138.* Coppola would keep his word.

3 On the Road

The Rain People

After *Finian's Rainbow,* Warner Bros., confident of the film's imminent success, offered Coppola $400,000 to direct another musical: *Mame.* But Coppola, being less optimistic, began having doubts about his capacity to direct this type of film. His lack of self-confidence made him wonder whether he would ever again be asked to direct valuable original screenplays. He feared that he was perhaps not as talented as he had once believed. He therefore decided to turn down all offers until he could prove himself to himself. He then concentrated on a project he had toyed with during his years of study and which would eventually become *The Rain People.*

He invested the money he had earned directing *Finian's Rainbow* and purchased eighty thousand dollars' worth of film equipment. He partially paid the actors and technicians. He actually invested every dollar he had in the production of *The Rain People.* But it was still not enough. Hence the reappearance of Warner Bros., who agreed to finance the rest of the film's expenses.

Coppola describes what followed: "This was perhaps in 1960. I had started to write a long screenplay entitled *The Gray Station Wagon.* I eventually changed the title to *Echoes.* It was the story of three women who decide to leave their respective husbands: a young woman who had been married just a few weeks earlier, a middle-aged woman with three children, and an older woman. I never finished it. I was about twenty-one at the time, and perhaps it was too ambitious an undertaking for me. Several years later, when I wanted to make a film based on my own material rather than an adaptation, I turned again to this old manuscript and decided to do the story of one of these women. And that is how *The Rain People* came about."

A Labor of Love

Coppola had always fantasized about writing a film tailored to a specific actress, "as Antonioni did for Monica Vitti." At that time, he greatly admired Shirley Knight, and met her at a film festival under the most extraordinary circumstances. "Shirley was crying because someone had spoken to her rudely. I went over to her and I said: 'Don't cry, I am going to write a film for you,' and she said: 'Oh really? That's nice!' "

The role of the young newlywed who runs away at dawn in her station wagon was thus written for her. She played the part of a pregnant young woman who turns her back on all the responsibilities that were being pushed on her. By leaving New York and heading west, she tries to put the greatest possible distance between herself and this existence she now rejects. "She got married, and suddenly she starts feeling that her personality is slipping away, without knowing why. What is the point of this marriage? What is her part in it?"

Coppola remembers with great emotion: "It was a labor of love. We had a very small crew traveling in a Dodge truck which we had modified to carry the most advanced film equipment available." He wrote the screenplay as they went along: "We made this film as we were crossing the United States in five cars and one truck, filming things as we saw them, choosing locations and even sequences as we came upon them." The cars and truck served as the studio, the cutting rooms, and the dressing rooms.

They began on Long Island, New York, and continued through eighteen states for eighteen weeks. There was never any advance preparation as they often stumbled upon sequences that would then be written into the film, such as the military parade in Chattanooga.

Unfortunately, the problems were caused not only by the constant moving around, but also by the difficult relationship between Shirley Knight and Francis Coppola. "Shirley is very

Desire. Robert Duvall and Shirley Knight in *The Rain People*. (Warner-Columbia Films) talented but she is the only actress with whom I did not really get along. Usually, I have a very good rapport with actors." The problem was, in fact, based on lack of trust and confidence. "I don't think that Shirley had confidence in me. I don't think she believed that, if she did what I said, this would turn out to be a good film."

Coppola describes in the following way the character of Natalie Ravenna played by Shirley Knight: "The woman I had in mind was much more schizophenic than it appears in the film. But she also had a terribly compassionate side. The basis of the character was her motherly instinct; she was a kind of mother figure. And I don't think I got that out of Shirley. I wanted to feel the nervous intensity of someone under pressure. I'm not sure how much I like the character I saw, whereas I loved the one I had written."

Because of his differences with his leading actress, Coppola modified his original idea and began placing more emphasis on the character played by James Caan. But he was not sure how to handle the complex role of Kilgannon, the overwrought football player who was as docile as a child. So he turned to the other roles, developing those of the police officer (Robert Duvall) and the animal breeder (Tom Aldredge).

But Coppola regretted not having perfected the part of Natalie Ravenna. He later said: "I think I am sincere enough to be able to put myself in the place of a woman, even though some say that is quite impossible. . . . I sensed that there must be married women who were expected to accomplish something, and who were in fact dying inside. I thought that it would be an interesting affirmation for one of them to simply get up and leave."

On the Road

The story begins on a rainy morning, in a quiet house on Long Island. Natalie Ravenna walks out of her house. In a note she leaves for her husband, she explains that she will return soon and that he should not worry about her. She gets into her station wagon, stops off to see her parents—who do not understand what she is doing—and leaves New York.

While traveling on the highways, she reflects upon her marriage and her role as a wife. She stops to call her husband and tell him of the obsessions that have been haunting her. He pleads with her to come home, but Natalie answers that she will come back only when she has made some sense of her feelings. She also tells him that she is pregnant.

She spends the night in a motel, then goes on. At one point, she stops to pick up a hitchhiker named Jimmy Kilgannon, nicknamed Killer. He had been a student at Helmont College, where he was a football hero. Now he is trying to get to West Virginia, where his former girlfriend's father has promised him a job. Night falls and they stop in another motel. They each take a room, but Killer comes into Natalie's room, where they dance and play "Simon Says." At one point, Natalie notices a metal plate on the young man's head. He explains that it was the result of a severe injury sustained during a football game. Natalie, who is moved by his story, gently sends him back to his room.

The next day, she decides to drive him to West Virginia. During the trip, Killer tells her the story of the Rain People: "They are made of rain. And when they cry they disappear altogether because they quite dissolve."

Natalie had intended to drop Killer off at his former girlfriend's home and go on. But when they arrive, the girlfriend explains to Natalie that Killer used to be a great champion who has become "slow" as a result of his accident. Natalie and Killer get back into the car and drive away. For a moment, Natalie considers abandoning her "big child." But she decides against it and they head for the Midwest.

Much later, Natalie finds a job for Killer on an animal farm in Ogallala, Nebraska. Suddenly overwhelmed by the caged animals around her, as they reflect her own feelings, she runs away and is stopped for speeding on the highway. She accompanies the officer, Gordon, to pay the fine. On their way, they stop at the animal farm, where Natalie learns that while she was away, Killer opened all the cages: he could not bear to see the animals locked up.

Natalie once again takes him under her wing. That same evening, she has a date with Gordon, the police officer. Before going out, she calls her husband, but Killer, in a childish gesture of jealousy, rips the telephone wires out of the wall. Natalie, furious, throws his bag out of the car and flees.

Natalie and Gordon spend the evening together and return to his mobile home. Gordon puts his little daughter, Rosalie, out of the camper. Natalie is shocked and wants to leave. But Gordon tells her to relax.

During this time, Killer has followed Natalie to the camper park, and he meets Rosalie, who is wandering about. The man who has remained a child and the child who grew up too quickly walk around together peering into the campers.

Meanwhile, Gordon is becoming more and more insistent and Natalie is about to give in to him when she changes her mind. He begins to threaten her, and she reaches for a gun, but he pushes her onto the bed. Killer, who has been watching through the window, breaks the door down and hits Gordon. Rosalie grabs the gun and shoots Killer, who collapses.

Natalie drags Killer to the car and swears to him that she will take care of him forever. But it is too late, and Killer is dead. Natalie sobs over his body.

In Search of an Identity

The main theme of *The Rain People* is a man's responsibility toward others, a subject that has always fascinated

The wanderer's agony. Shirley Knight in *The Rain People*. (Warner-Columbia Films)

Coppola. In this case, Natalie's responsibility toward her husband, toward her unborn child, toward the injured football player, and finally toward the traumatized police officer. Natalie comes into contact with all of these people and is called upon to take care of them when she is incapable of taking care of herself. Subconsciously, and eventually consciously, she has left her husband in search of a lover, "just someone new to make love with," as she tells Killer in a moment of anger. She wants to escape from the sudden and overwhelming responsibility of this child she is carrying. But she ends up caring for a man who has remained a child and is, in fact, the embodiment of the baby she refuses to acknowledge or accept.

Coppola confirms this: "He is a metaphor of the child she is carrying. She is like a woman driving around and talking to her unborn child and telling him: 'How can I take care of you when I can hardly take care of myself?' At the same time, she already feels a strong and sincere attachment to him."

As in all of Coppola's films, the opening scene is a winner: it is a pure, sensual, stunning marvel! There is no music. Just the far-off humming of a sanitation truck.

From the very start, Coppola sets the color of the film: it is a gray rainy morning in suburbia. *The Rain People* are here, in this quiet house on Long Island.

An empty swing moves ever so slightly under the raindrops. We will think back on this swing, as the place where the unborn child will eventually play.

As the end of the film, there is another swing, with another child in it: Rosalie, who rocks back and forth frenetically, sitting across from Gordon, another grown-up child, whom she will soon kill in what is a strange filial struggle and a sudden revelation of feelings that had been repressed until then.

And in between these two sequences, Coppola speaks to us softly.

Rage and tears. Shirley Knight and James Caan in *The Rain People*. (Warner-Columbia Films)

Or rather, not at all. He becomes our eyes and our ears. His camera takes us on a long journey on America's highways, on a flight whose purpose is not clear. In spite of the note left for her husband and the brief stop at her parents' house, Natalie never explains her reasons for leaving. There is no thesis, no antithesis, and no synthesis. Fear and flight are, by definition, illogical and frantic.

We slip into the comfort and security of the station wagon in which Natalie seems like a little girl who has secretly borrowed her parents' car. She is alone on this endless road. But she has chosen to be so. It is perhaps the only decision she has ever made consciously. She simply got up quietly, took a shower, and walked away from a situation that had become like a prison to her.

She goes straight, heading west, the only possible direction of escape from where she is living.

Only on these cold and endless turnpikes does the music appear, in our minds as well as in Natalie's, bringing with it rushes of memories. She hums a few notes in her motel room. She is alone. The ballad is superb, melancholic, and obsessive, with the unmistakable feel of a child's lullaby.

The camera then becomes airborne, offering a dazzling counterpoint image of the fleeing car, heading full speed down the highways of the Midwest. The camera circles over it, closing in lovingly, following it tenderly. Then, it suddenly stops and we see a hitchhiker. Natalie wants to stop for him, hesitates, decides against it, goes on, then stops again. And Coppola offers us a magical shot of a red sunset, the first of many sunset shots to come. And again the nostalgic "road music."

This student, who is leaving his college, was a former football hero. He is rather good-looking and well-built. We can actually feel Natalie's interest in Kilgannon (Killer). At first she lies to him, telling him her name is Sara.

She is denying her true identity, that of a married and pregnant woman, what she was before she escaped. During her telephone conversation with her husband, she has said: "She, I, your wife . . ." Was that a voluntary effort to put distance between them or a quest for a new and more satisfactory identity? Probably a little of both.

James Caan as the enigmatic narrator of *The Rain People*. (Warner-Columbia Films)

Only What Is Essential

Given her fervent desire to "know" a new man, Natalie tries to become a new woman. But the man turns out to be a child. The injured Killer is docile and obedient. We do, however, question the reason behind his answer when Natalie asks him why he always does what he is told. He replies: "I don't know, it's easier that way." Why is it easier? we wonder.

This uncertainty as to his possible motivation appears again when Natalie and Killer stop at his former girlfriend's house. Natalie asks him again: "You can tell me now, you'll probably never see me again. You pretend to be unresponsive to what you hear, you pretend, right?" His impenetrable and steady gaze along with his impassive half-smile only serve to reinforce our doubt.

Is he or is he not pretending? Is it easier to appear strange than to struggle with normalcy? Does Killer realize that by remaining a child he can avoid the wounds of time and the heavy responsibilities that come with being an adult? Is he fleeing from the same things as Natalie? We will never know. Coppola cleverly avoids furnishing us with any definitive answer, thus leaving us with several possible interpretations of the character. Killer finds in Natalie the comforting mother figure he has lost. She becomes his sister, his impossible lover, his friend. "My only friend," says Killer, when talking of her to the farm owner.

For Natalie, he is an acceptable version of the child she fears. On several occasions, she will abandon him and turn her back on the truth, but the truth is inescapable.

The feeling of freedom she senses on the open highways is just a mirage. One cannot escape from oneself by running away. Slowly and surreptitiously, the feelings she so fears begin growing in her for this being who is even more fragile than she, and who clings to her tenderness.

These rain people, whom Killer describes to her, are right before our eyes. There is a subtle and marvelous sequence of shots in which Coppola shows us these two people alternately from inside and outside the car. Outside, the rain bathes the car in darkness, while the windshield wipers mark the rhythm of Killer's story. This strange story of the rain people leaves Natalie pensive. Is it true, do they exist? It is true, answers Killer. Have you ever seen them? Once. What are they like? They look like everybody else, except the woman is very beautiful, and so is the man. And they are made of rain. . . . That's all. Nothing else will be said. We are left to wonder.

In truth, the rain people are more numerous than one might think. Gordon, the tough macho police officer, is actually traumatized by the death of his wife. He pretends that he no longer loved her at the time when the fire broke out. But his memories, seen in flashbacks, belie what he says. We see him sobbing over her dead body. There is an unmistakable similarity between that scene and the one of Natalie lying over Killer's body at the end of the film.

The poster for the film claimed that "rain people are very fragile. One mistake in love and they dissolve. . . ."

As a "personal" film (screenplay, dialogue), *The Rain People* remains Coppola's favorite. It was undoubtedly the most influential and moving work of his early career. The importance of this film will be attested by the many references made to it in all of Coppola's later works.

The Actors in the Rain

The actors' performances were outstanding, especially that of James Caan, who claims to this day that it was the finest performance of his career. The American critics called it his best role in ten years. Caan considers *The Rain People* to be one of his favorite films, and believes that Francis Coppola is "probably the greatest film director in the world."

The experience of this film sealed for the two men a friendship that had begun at Hofstra College. They would collaborate again in *The Godfather*.

Shirley Knight, who had been praised for her performances in Richard Brooks's *Sweet Bird of Youth* and Sidney Lumet's *The Group*, drew admiration for her portrayal of Natalie. She brings reality, dramatic intensity, weakness, and strength to the part; she gives her character a human dimension that is quite moving and conveys a sense of universality. As for Robert Duvall, who plays the part of the police officer, this was his first meeting with Coppola, who eventually chose him to play Don Corleone's lawyer in *The Godfather* and Colonel Kilgore in *Apocalypse Now* ("I love the smell of napalm in the morning"). As Gordon, he is in turn impressive, funny, ridiculous, and moving. The police officer is also one of the *Rain People*. And Robert Duvall is one of America's greatest contemporary actors.

A Soul of Velvet

The Rain People won the grand prize for Best Film at the international festival at San Sebastian in 1969, and Coppola won the award for Best Director.

The critics were, for the most part, favorably impressed. Henry Rabine (*La Croix*) expressed his enthusiasm in this way: "I liked Francis Ford Coppola's film very much. It is a gentle film, with muted colors, tender gestures, quiet moments and details. A secret film in which a heart beats quietly. Coppola works with discretion, with understatement, with a soul of velvet. His film is ineffable, and what is important is what is not said. It is a story of people looking for each other without finding each other. Time floats around them, incapable of bringing them any closer to each other. Hence the empty moments, the pauses during which nothing happens while despair slowly moves in. The only hope to be found is in life itself."

An act of deliverance. James Caan in *The Rain People*. (Warner-Columbia Films)

A scene from *The Rain People* that was cut from the final version. (Warner-Columbia Films)

25

In her book *Hollywood Renaissance,* Diane Jacobs writes: "In my opinion, *The Rain People* is not only a lovely film to watch, but it is also one the deepest studies about responsibility and independence, about the moral implications and the ambiguities of love and sin, ever brought to the screen. . . . It depicts an eternal existential dilemma with feeling and insight. . . ."

If *The Rain People* is an imperfect film, as Coppola himself will point out, it is assuredly his most perfect "imperfect" one.

Lucas Films Coppola

This chapter would be incomplete if we did not include a few words concerning the activities of Georges Lucas during the filming of *The Rain People*. Hired as Coppola's assistant (ever since *Finian's Rainbow*), Lucas came across a film camera that was not being used. He asked permission to use it, thinking that, if Coppola could direct "a small film on the intimate lives of real people, [he, Lucas], could make a small film in the style of the cinéma verité, a kind of cinematographic journal on the real lives of the people making *The Rain People.*" The result was *Filmmaker,* "a documentary that offers a personal viewpoint on the daily tensions and stress occurring during a film production."

Coppola incorporated the budget for this film into that intended for location stills. But the main direction given Lucas was to stay out of everyone's way. Lucas thus had twelve thousand dollars with which to prepare this thirty-minute documentary. He filmed the stormy confrontations which occurred between Coppola and Shirley Knight. But in the final cut, he decided to leave them out, so as "not to damage anyone's career," he explains.

As a privileged witness to this memorable filming event, Lucas added a few details about the working conditions during the odyssey across the United States. He remembers it as one of the best times of his life. "We really did have a good time during that trip. It was difficult, but for the young

Violence and passion. To protect her father, Robert Duvall, Marya Zimmet kills James Caan. (Warner-Columbia Films)

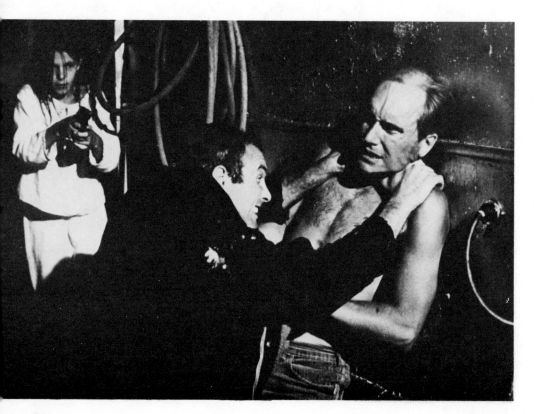

The tenderness between father and daughter. (Warner-Columbia Films)

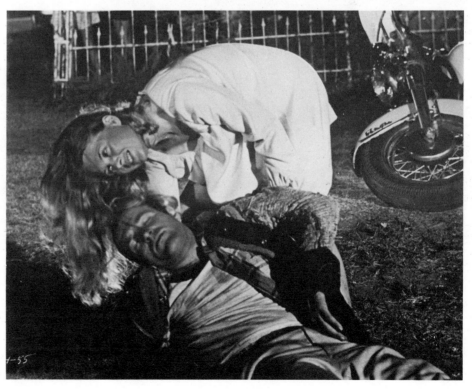

Natalie tries to comfort "Killer," but it is too late. The end. (Warner-Columbia Films)

Top: **Shirley Knight and Robert Duvall in *The Rain People*.** (Warner-Columbia Films)

Bottom: **A momentary dizzy spell that masks a deeper problem.** (Warner-Columbia Films)

clowns that we were, it was fun." Lucas was particularly impressed by Coppola's respect for artistic freedom and the enthusiastic all-for-one-and-one-for-all attitude which he generally exhibited during the filming. Coppola gave each member of the crew "unofficial certificates that could be traded in for original certificates good for one percent of the net profits of the film." But the film did not show any net profits.

The living conditions in the different shooting locations (eighteen different states!) were often the source of further tensions among the crew members. The twenty-three people who formed the group spent "countless nights in Howard Johnson motels located in the middle of nowhere. It was nerve-wracking," says Lucas.

A rather amusing episode occurred when they were in the Southwest. The crew members, including Lucas and Coppola, were forced to shave their beards because "long-haired hippies" were not at all welcome in those traditional southern states. What was surprising was that "Coppola was unrecognizable without his beard, and no one would listen to him," remembers Lucas.

The future director of *Star Wars* also captured a rare moment on film: that of Coppola's spontaneous creativity as he frenetically rewrote scripts as they went along, particularly during their stay in Chattanooga, when Coppola decided to write in the military parade scene upon which they had accidentally stumbled. Coppola, who was suffering from the flu at that point, spent a great deal of time in the bathroom of the Greyhound bus terminal. Because of this, he decided to use it as a location for a key scene of the film, the one where Killer is sitting on his suitcase and waiting—before Natalie returns to get him.

Finally, there is one essential phrase uttered by Coppola in front of Lucas's camera that bears repeating. During a heated telephone conversation between Coppola and one of the heads of

Warner Bros., Coppola suddenly shouted: "The system will collapse under its own weight! It cannot fail to do so!" This was in 1969. Fifteen years later, when he had reached the peak of success, Coppola still maintains the same claim: "Our cinema was the best in the world. We had the best set designers, the best workmen, disciplined actors. In twenty years, we destroyed everything . . . without anyone realizing what was happening. Today, Hollywood is a giant television industry. People who control the cinema don't like it anymore."

American Zoetrope

"The main objective of this company will be to undertake film production in several different areas by collaborating with the most gifted and talented young people, using the most contemporary and sophisticated equipment available." (Press release announcing the formation of American Zoetrope.)

This vision was, if not utopian, at least very romantic: a film community made up of participants under the age of thirty offering a different approach to that of the sterile and profligate Hollywood.

It was to be a privileged place where young, inexperienced film directors could learn the Coppolian philosophy according to which "film is the ultimate form of expression."

This dream began to take form during the filming of *The Rain People*. While in Nebraska, the actors and the crew were discussing a simple concept: "making films anywhere, without having to answer to a large studio." Coppola remembers: "We had fantasized about going out to San Francisco, where we would be free to make films the way we had made *The Rain People*." After delivering the completed film to Warner Bros., Coppola traveled to Scandinavia, where he visited Lantern Films, a small Danish film studio that owned the most complete collection of magic lanterns

and old projectors. Coppola was struck by the costly equipment he saw there. "I thought that new technology would be the magic ingredient for our success. We all had this naïve notion back then that the equipment would give us the means of production. We were wrong. Money does."

On his way home, Coppola stopped off at the commercial fair in Cologne and ordered eighty thousand dollars' worth of equipment, including a complete mixing studio. He had no money, no place to put this equipment, and, more importantly, no film to make. In June of 1969, Coppola, George Lucas, Ron Colby, and Mona Skager arrived in San Francisco seeking to create the exact equivalent of Lantern Films. They had already decided on a name for their future company, which reflected its Danish influence: Zoetrope (a system for projecting moving images by means of a rotating cylinder). Coppola had been given one of these as a gift. Also the Greek root of the word meant "the movement of life," a symbol perfectly adapted to the new community.

After a few arguments between Lucas and Coppola concerning their respective ideas of what their new venture should be (Coppola wanted Zoetrope to be an all-encompassing studio, complete with a landing strip for helicopters and parking facilities for mobile studios, whereas Lucas simply wanted "a nice little house to work in"), they moved American Zoetrope into a former warehouse at 827 Folsom Street.

The Way of the Future

They thought they had reached their goal, according to Ron Colby: "We wanted to avoid the depressing atmosphere of Hollywood. We felt it was judicious to leave it behind and become autonomous. We did not have the feeling, each day, of clocking in at the factory. And, in any case, it was our factory."

Coppola wanted to make Zoetrope the new elite of the film industry. Lucas noted jokingly that their group resembled *The Dirty Dozen,* as the original four members were soon joined by Caroll Ballard, Hal Barwood, John Korty, Willard Huyck, Gloria Katz, John Milius, Matthew Robbins, and Martin Scorsese.

The location was far from sumptuous, and the equipment arrived from Germany while they were in the middle of construction. "It was like at Christmas, when you're trying to assemble a bicycle before the children wake up, and you have to hurry to put all the pieces together, and it all goes wrong because the instructions are missing," says Lucas, remembering the first days at Zoetrope.

On November 19, 1969, Coppola incorporated the new company under the name American Zoetrope (Lucas had proposed Transamerican Sprocket Works!).

Coppola was the president (and the only shareholder), Lucas the vice-president, and Mona Skager the secretary-treasurer.

There was little money at first, but they anticipated incoming funds thanks to the release of *The Rain People*. The project began to attract many professionals, along with those who were just beginning: Stanley Kubrick and Coppola exchanged weekly letters concerning the techniques used in *2001: A Space Odyssey*. John Schlesinger was also interested in the group. Mike Nichols wanted to invest in American Zoetrope. And Orson Welles went into negotiations with the company for the possible production of a film which was never made.

"Francis would have given a camera to a street cleaner who expressed an interest in the company," says Lucas. It was a euphoric time during which a screenwriter would be hired practically on the spot and a director would be taken on after a quick glimpse at his twelve-minute student project.

Lucas was more reticent. "Francis

thought of Zoetrope as a sort of alternative studio in the way of *Easy Rider*. He envisioned it as a place where he would gather many young talented people who would work for free, producing films with the hope that one of these would be a hit. In this manner, the film studio would grow."

Coppola's enthusiasm was the company's driving force, sweeping over the pessimism or discontent of others. And the word soon spread, from UCLA to USC, that Zoetrope was the way of the future.

Black Thursday

Coppola offered Warner Bros. a total of seven film projects, including *THX 1138,* based on a short film by Lucas, and *Apocalypse Now,* conceived by John Milius and George Lucas. Warner Bros. agreed, and *THX 1138* was the first film to be produced by Zoetrope. Coppola proudly made the announcement to Lucas, who was displeased by the fact that Coppola had not consulted him about *Apocalypse Now* before making the deal with Warner Bros. "But we really had the feeling that Zoetrope was going to be *big,* and that we, the young film directors, were going to conquer the world."

Lucas was paid only fifteen thousand dollars to write and direct *THX 1138.* He was consoled by the fact that he would earn twenty-five thousand dollars for *Apocalypse Now.*

The problems began as soon as the filming of *THX 1138* was completed. When the heads of Warner Bros. saw the film, they were aghast and did not understand it at all. They immediately called in a Warner Bros. veteran, Rudi Fehr, to recut the film. Still dissatisfied, Warner Bros. canceled all future projects with Zoetrope, including *The Conversation* and *Apocalypse Now.*

It was a sinister day for Zoetrope, one that would go down in its history as the Black Thursday, reminiscent of that Black Tuesday of the stock market crash in 1929. But even more problems were looming on the horizon: "My enthusiasm and my imagination had simply gone beyond any financial logic," admits Coppola. He also realized that there was no real coherent philosophical link betwen himself and the other members of the company. "The only prinicple was that of freedom and of young directors; that was vague, very vague."

The liberty actually went a little too far. "Some people borrowed or simply stole our equipment. We lost nearly four thousand dollars' worth of equipment during the first year, not to mention all the damaged cars. It was utter madness."

Lucas and Coppola were crushed by Warner Bros.' withdrawal. All their hopes had crumbled in one fell swoop, one sad Thursday in June 1970. It also represented a loss of approximately three hundred thousand dollars: the amount the studios had invested to pay for the screenplays.

Coppola bounced back quickly and tried to meet his most pressing debts. Zoetrope diversified and began producing television commercials and several educational films. In spite of these efforts, American Zoetrope remained in the red.

But Coppola soon had a moment of respite, as *Patton* became enormously successful. Coppola, along with Edmund H. North, had written the screenplay for Franklin Schaffner's film, which was, along with *Love Story,* the biggest hit of 1970.

George C. Scott was awarded an Oscar (which he promptly refused) for his performance in the title role. The film had been written in 1966 (when Coppola was twenty-seven years old), and although Coppola had a limited military experience, he had researched the subject thoroughly. He was reserved in his opinion of the general: "Patton was obviously out of his mind, and if a film were made about him praising him to the heavens, it would undoubtedly make everyone laugh. But, at the same time, the producers would have turned down a script that would have been too negative." Coppola decided to focus on the duality of this character, to show him as "a man out of touch with his time, a pathetic hero, a kind of Don Quixote." Everyone could then find a facet in him that interested him. And that was the key to the success of the film.

Coppola's original screenplay, written in six months, was rewritten on several occasions. But George C. Scott refused to make the film with any other screenplay than Coppola's. That version became the final one, with a few modifications made by Edmund H. North.

George Lucas in 1968, shooting *Filmmaker*.

The Corleones, father and sons: James Caan, Marlon Brando, Al Pacino, and John Cazale.

4 The Power and the Glory

The Godfather

While mired in the financial problems caused by Warner Bros.' withdrawal of financial support, Coppola received a telephone call from Paramount, offering him, once again, the opportunity to direct *The Godfather.* He had already declined once, six months earlier, when he could hardly get through the first fifty pages of Mario Puzo's book, calling it "cheap and sensational." If he eventually accepted the job of directing "this gangster movie," it was because George Lucas had convinced him of their desperate need for money to finance their own projects.

Coppola then carefully reread the book and saw its potential: It was "a story about a family, about a father and his sons, about power and succession, a formidable subject as long as you eliminated everything else." He added that "not only could it be a hit, it could also be a good film."

Coppola adds modestly that "if both *Godfather*s worked, it was because Mario Puzo wrote a strong and realistic book, with all the key elements included."

All the rights to the film had been sold before the book became a bestseller. Mario Puzo (who had spent three years finishing the book) had not thought of adapting it for the 'screen until he read in a newspaper that Danny Thomas wanted to play the part of Don Corleone. Puzo jumped at this, because he had always envisioned Marlon Brando in the title role. Through a common friend, Jeff Brown, he was able to reach Brando, who warned that "the studio would never hire him unless it was at the request of the director."

But Paramount, who owned the rights to *The Godfather*, and had just recently been burned by the failure of another Mafia film, *The Brotherhood*, had no intention of producing this film.

Only when the book became a bestseller did Paramount ask Puzo to write the screenplay. He refused at first, because of the insufficient salary they offered. Paramount was intending this to be a low-budget film. Puzo and Paramount finally agreed on a percentage system and signed a contract. Once in Hollywood, Puzo expressed his desire to have Marlon Brando play the title role, but Paramount gave him no answer. Puzo was working on the second draft of the screenplay when Coppola agreed to direct the film.

One might wonder why Paramount chose Coppola, whose commercial value at the time was not very high. Perhaps his Italian name had something to do with it, given the pressure that was being exerted by Italian-American groups upon learning of the film's production. An Italian director might soothe some of the tensions that were rising. Puzo believes they chose Coppola because "he was under thirty, his last two films had failed, and therefore they thought they could control him." As for Coppola, he attributed their choice to the facts that many directors, such as Costa-Gavras and Richard Brooks, had turned down the project, that the book had not yet become a best-seller, and that he, Coppola, had the reputation of directing films for little money. Most of all, Paramount never anticipated the fact that *The Godfather* would become a blockbuster!

"I Want to Look Like a Bulldog"

The projected budget was not to exceed one million dollars. As it turned out, *The Godfather*'s final budget was over five million dollars!

At first, Coppola and Puzo worked separately, each one rereading and correcting the other's work. The two men got along very well and Mario Puzo insisted that Coppola share the credit for the final version of the screenplay.

But what really brought them together was their common desire to have Marlon Brando play the leading role. "Francis is a bon vivant, he is even-tempered and pleasant. I never knew he could be that inflexible when it came to work: he fought and he succeeded in getting them to accept Brando," says Puzo.

Coppola had, nevertheless, auditioned over two thousand actors for the part. He saw all the older Italian actors, but none of them were right for the part. It became obvious that "the role had to go to an actor with incontestable magnetism, an actor who would create a stir simply by walking into a room." That left only the two best actors in the world, Laurence Olivier and Marlon Brando.

But Paramount refused to commit itself. Meanwhile, the book's success was growing, "it was getting bigger than me," says Coppola, "and Paramount was beginning to wonder if they had not made a mistake in choosing me."

As Paramount still refused to make a decision concerning Brando, Coppola refused to go any further. Stanley Jaffe, the president of Paramount, organized a meeting during which he told Coppola: "I assure you, as president of this company, that Marlon Brando will not appear in this film, and I will not allow you to bring the matter up again." Brando had been classified as "box-office poison" ever since the failure of *Mutiny on the Bounty*.

But Coppola persevered and was allowed to voice his demand one last time. "I got up, as if I were about to defend a man condemned to death, and I listed the reasons that made Brando irreplaceable, one of them being that he had an aura about him, when he was surrounded by other actors, similar to that of Don Corleone with his people." To add strength to his argument, Coppola then pretended to faint before the representatives of the film studio!

Paramount authorized Coppola to consider Marlon Brando for the part on three conditions: that Brando submit to a screen test, that he not be paid to do so, and that Brando guarantee, with his own money, that the film would not go over the anticipated bud-

get. Actually, Brando would receive a percentage of the film's profits and would not suffer from the arrangement.

Coopola was terrified at the thought of asking Brando to do a screen test, but Brando offered to do so even before Coppola asked. The very next day, Coppola, a cameraman, and Salvatore Corsitto, who would read with Brando, went to see him. "Brando received us in his living room," Coppola recounts, "wearing a Japanese kimono and a ponytail. As soon as I began recording he slipped into the character's skin. He put a little shoe polish on his hair and some Kleenex in his mouth: 'I want to look like a bulldog,' he said, and began to improvise." Coppola was amazed to see Brando, who was then forty-seven years old, metamorphose, right before his eyes, into the head of the Mafia. When he showed the reel to Stanley Jaffe and Robert Evans, both agreed that Brando's performance was the work of a "genius."

Although the casting of the other parts was simple enough, with James Caan and Robert Duvall breezing through their screen tests, the part of Michael remained unassigned. They wanted someone "chic," distinguished, Ivy League. Al Pacino, who was the first choice of Coppola and Puzo, seemed too short and too Italian to play the part of the "American in the family." But Coppola insisted that "a good actor is a good actor." During the screen test, Pacino did not know his lines, but Coppola, headstrong, made him repeat them all day long. In spite of his efforts, the screen test was not convincing. There was talk of pushing back the first day of shooting, while Coppola alone still wanted Pacino for the part. Finally, it was agreed: Pacino would play Michael.

Against Paramount's wishes, Brando returned to England to finish filming *The Nightcomers*. Coppola followed him there. During the day, Brando would work on his film while Coppola worked on the screenplay; in the evening, they discussed the char-

acter of Don Corleone and how he should be interpreted.

The shoot finally began in early 1971. Coppola had decided to start with the scene of the meeting which takes place in the offices of the Corleone olive oil importing company. As it did not go quite right, Brando suggested more rehearsals, but Coppola refused, knowing that he was being watched by the producers and already behind schedule. When he looked at the rushes, he saw his mistake and asked to shoot the scene once more. The Paramount people were beginning to wonder whether Coppola was too young and inexperienced to handle the situation.

That was not all. Several of the technicians, specifically the camerman, were especially unpleasant if not downright insulting to Coppola. The budget increased daily, and when Coppola asked for twenty-seven additional shooting days, he was refused them. With very little discretion, Robert Evans asked whether Elia Kazan was available to direct the film. "They all felt that Kazan was the only director in the world who could work with Brando," complains Coppola, who began having nightmares. "I couldn't sleep anymore. I kept dreaming that Kazan would arrive on the set and would say to me 'Uh, Francis, I've been asked to . . . ' But Marlon, who knew about this, was very supportive, and said he would not continue to work on the film if I were fired."

So Coppola continued shooting, with the omnipresent threat of finding himself replaced for the very three reasons that eventually made the film a success: his insistence on having Brando play the lead, then his insistence on Pacino, and finally his most audacious requirement, his insistence that part of the film be shot in Sicily. But Coppola stood firm. Among other things, he demanded that certain uncooperative members of the crew be fired, which did not stop them from spreading rumors that "*The Godfather* was on its way toward being the worst disaster of all time. . . ."

The head of the family, Marlon Brando.

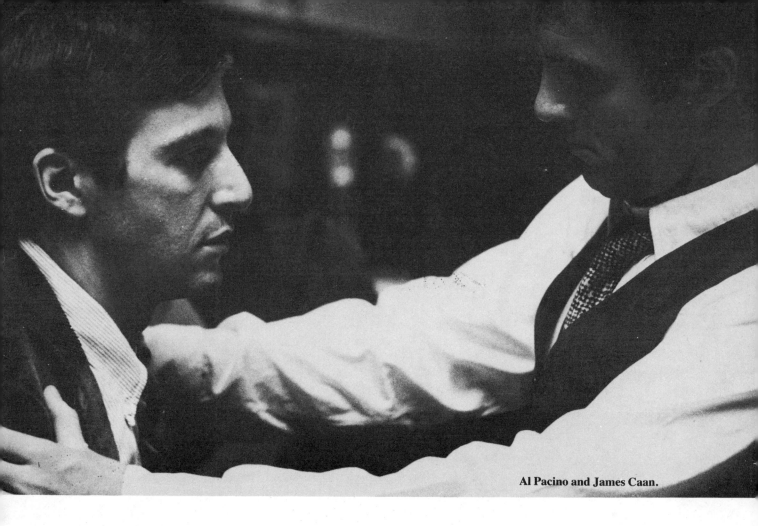

Al Pacino and James Caan.

The Godfather Is Dead, Long Live the Godfather

The film traces the story of Don Vito Corleone, the head of one of the five Italian-American "families" that rule organized crime. It is 1945 and Don Vito, in the famous opening sequence, is celebrating the wedding of his daughter Connie to Carlo Rizzi. Connie's three brothers, Sonny, Michael, and Freddie, are present at the reception. Michael, who has never participated in the family "business," takes this opportunity to introduce his friend Kay Adams to the rest of the family. Don Vito, who is the true center of attraction at the reception, receives the homage of all the guests during the course of the afternoon. Some come to congratulate him on the marriage of his daughter, while others thank him for a favor he has done for them. Johnny Fontane, an entertainer, asks

for his help in obtaining a part in a film that will be produced by Jack Woltz. Woltz has already turned Fontane down. Don Corleone sends Tom Hagen, his right-hand man, to discuss the matter with Woltz, who refuses to change his mind. One morning soon thereafter, Woltz wakes to find the head of his favorite horse on his bed. (Many viewers deplored the fate of the horse "more than they did the fate of the many people killed during the film," says Coppola. To reassure these viewers, Coppola explained that everything had been done according to the rules: the head of the animal had been brought to the set "on ice," the scene had been shot in the presence of members of the ASPCA, and the head was returned at the end of the shooting sequence.)

Shortly after this scene, during another reunion, the representatives of the other "families" invite Don Corleone to participate in several drug

transactions. He refuses to go along, claiming that it would result in the disruption of the existing peace between the families and certain influential political figures. Sonny openly disagrees with his father. Sollozzo, the head of one of the families, concludes that the only solution is to assassinate Don Corleone. He is shot five times, but not killed.

Michael, visiting his father in the hospital, discovers the existence of a new plot to eliminate Don Corleone. Unarmed, he is able nevertheless to foil the attempt on his father's life. McClumskey, a police officer who, with Sollozzo, had planned the assassination attempt, is furious and beats up Michael. Michael decides to avenge his father and the affront he has sustained. After making an appointment with the two men in a restaurant, he shoots both of them with a gun he had hidden in the men's room, and thus enters the "family" life. But he is forced to leave the country. In Sicily, where he has gone, he marries Apollonia, a beautiful local girl. His enemies soon discover his whereabouts and place a bomb in his car. The explosion will kill Apollonia. Meanwhile, back in the United States, Carlo Rizzi has betrayed Sonny, who is killed.

The aging Don tries to arrange a truce, and agrees to let Michael, who has since returned to the United States and married Kay, become more involved in the family's activities.

The Don retires and dies shortly thereafter of a heart attack during one of the film's most gripping scenes—a scene that Coppola did not know how to film. He wanted to give the scene credibility by including the Don's grandson. "Brando said to me, 'This is how I play with children.' And he took an orange peel cut out in the shape of fangs and stuffed it in his mouth." Coppola, who was surprised at first, understood Brando's idea: the Godfather dies as a monster would. "After having seen him like that, I couldn't film the scene any other way."

The film bounces back from this point, as Michael plans the total extermination of his enemies, including his brother-in-law Rizzi. During the massacre, Michael is in church, attending the christening of his niece (the daughter of Connie and Rizzi), to whom he is godfather. In a moment of rage, Connie accuses him of having murdered her husband. Kay, who is present, asks Michael whether this is true, but Michael denies any participation in the matter. As Kay leaves the room, closing the door behind her, she sees all of the Godfather's men regrouping around Michael and informing him of the success of the operation and congratulating him. The Godfather is dead, long live the Godfather.

Once filming was completed, Coppola still faced problems with its length. To comply with the studio's wishes, he was prepared to cut fifteen minutes, even though he did not wish to do so. But Robert Evans, who had decided that the film would undoubt-

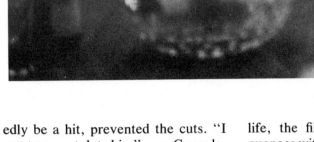

Marlon Brando, the Godfather, with Robert Duvall.

edly be a hit, prevented the cuts. "I must congratulate him" says Coppola. "After seeing the film, he fought to keep it in its entire length."

Although Coppola was not responsible for all the decisions which made *The Godfather* the blockbuster that it was (in the first months following its release, in March 1972, it earned over a million dollars a day), he was directly responsible for the film's quality.

As the film's director, and in spite of all the production difficulties, Coppola was able to recreate faithfully the atmosphere of an important time in American history. "My Italian heritage helped me a great deal," he admits. "I had decided to include all of the Catholic rituals in this film. Hence the final scene of the baptism. I know every detail of such rituals and I had never seen a film that really captured the essence of what it was like to be an Italian-American."

As a perfect metaphor of American life, the film alternates violent sequences with more peaceful ones.

A constant undercurrent of violence occurs throughout the film, which presents by turns scenes that show the threat of violence, the fear of violence, the actual violent act, and then its repercussions.

The film offers hallucinatory murder scenes of intense visual strength. Can one ever forget the sight of Carlo Rizzi trying desperately to break the windshield of the car in which he is being asphyxiated? Or Brasi's impaled hand? Or Michael putting a bullet through McClumskey's head? Or Moe Greene's broken glasses?

This omnipresent violence is unforgettable, and is intended to draw a parallel between the Mafia and the United States. As Rap Brown said, "Violence is as American as cherry pie." Coppola developed this idea, explaining that "both the Mafia and the United States had their roots in Europe and both bear the traces of blood spilled to protect their power and insure their interests. Both also believe in a capitalist way of life, whose goal is profit."

This violence is balanced by Don Vito Corleone's family life. He is not a Scarface in flashy suits and monogrammed shirts, but a quiet "homebody," often seen shopping or playing with his grandson. He is a man who has reached the end of his life, a tired man with a gray beard wearing rumpled clothes . . . Coppola admits to having shown an implacable side of the Mafia (whose name is never once mentioned during the film). The charisma of the main characters generally overshadowed the film's moral implications. In the closing scene of the film, Michael has all of his enemies executed and lies to his wife as he closes the door behind her. Coppola would strive to correct this when he undertook the filming of *The Godfather, Part II*.

The World Is Theirs

After the success of *The Godfather,* Coppola resumed his experiments with his global vision of the cinema.

In 1972, he founded the Directors Company under the auspices of Paramount. The main partners included, besides Coppola, Peter Bogdanovich and William Friedkin, two directors who were very much in demand at the time. Each of them agreed to make four films within the next twelve years. Paramount would distribute these films in exchange for financial support in the amount of $31,500,000.

The Directors Company was responsible for the creation of three films before disappearing: *The Conversation,* by Coppola, and *Paper Moon* and *Daisy Miller,* by Peter Bogdanovich.

Coppola played an important role in the financing of George Lucas's project *American Graffiti.* At the time, none of the studios were interested in producing the film. But Coppola made an arrangement with Universal—which put up the one million dollars needed by Lucas—to be the film's executive producer and to direct a film for the studio. In return, Coppola would receive a percentage of the film's profits, which were, to everyone's surprise, considerable.

He came to Lucas's aid once again during a disagreement between Lucas and Universal on how the film should be cut. Coppola's intervention resulted in Lucas securing the right to cut the film as he wished.

On March 27, 1973, Coppola appeared before television audiences during the Academy Awards when *The Godfather* won the Oscar for Best Film. He was awarded an Oscar for Best Screenplay (in collaboration with Mario Puzo) and Marlon Brando was named Best Actor for his interpretation of Don Corleone.

It was a heady time for these young film directors. Coppola was the first among them to score a great commercial success. Other members of this new elite included John Milius (*Dillinger*), John Hancock (*Bang the Drum Slowly*), Martin Scorsese (*Mean Streets*), and Noel Black (*Pretty Poison*). In their newfound glory, these young mavericks were convinced that the world was about to be theirs.

Cinema 5

Coppola began investing the colossal sums of money he had earned from *The Godfather.* The magnitude of his investments was, as always, commensurate with the size of his projects. He acquired a huge house and an apartment in San Francisco. He purchased the Little Fox Theater, where he hoped to establish his own company. He bought several homes in an area of Mill Valley for his screenwriters and other associates. He invested in one of Los Angeles's most beautiful palaces, Marmont Castle on Sunset Boulevard, and in Goldwyn studios, where he opened his own offices.

In 1974, he bought a controlling interest in Cinema 5, Donald Rogoff's distribution company that specialized in foreign films. Coppola, who was planning eventually to distribute his own films through the channels of Cinema 5, named one of his own companies Cinema 7. As he had dreamed, he was on his way to establishing a viable alternative to the large studios for film distribution.

During this time, Coppola turned his interest and attention to other forms of media. He invested in television, radio, and the San Francisco–based *City Magazine.* During the first six months of his active participation, the magazine's circulation increased by fifty percent, but nevertheless kept losing money (nearly thirty thousand dollars per issue). Coppola soon returned to the cinema. By the start of 1976 he was deep at work on the preparations for his next film, *Apocalypse Now.* Needing money, he sold his shares in Cinema 5, shut down his Los Angeles offices, and mortgaged his holdings.

The Dream Is Over

In 1975, while he was still investing, Coppola had confided in Fred Roos: "I will probably go bankrupt in a few years and find myself back at square one, so I might as well enjoy myself now."

While he was filming *Apocalypse Now,* his concern for Zoetrope mounted. In April 1977, Coppola dreamt that his experience had ended in failure. The concept had been an excellent and ambitious one. But his being so far away, in the Philippines, and the inevitable problems of shooting on location, all contributed to his discontent. He wrote a long letter, expressing both his anger and his sorrow, to the attention of his employees and associates who had remained in the States. Although the tone of the letter was anguished, the message was clear: the dream was over. Coppola set down a new set of rules and regulations: all extravagance would cease, expenditures would henceforth have to be submitted and approved, the staff "should dress and behave as they

Paying respect to the Don.

would in any other company," and, he added, "it is essential to dispel the hippie-like ambience that has reigned here for the past seven years." But the main thrust of his message was that, following the completion of projects in progress, Caroll Ballard's **The Black Stallion** and Wim Wenders's **Hammett**, American Zoetrope would devote itself exclusively to the works of Francis Coppola. In other words, the dream of a community of film directors had failed.

As a final point, Francis Ford Coppola was to be, from that point on, Francis Coppola—consistent with his own principle of never trusting a man with three names!

This revealing document was published in *Esquire* magazine and facetiously entitled: "Case History of Business: Hollywood Artistic Division."

In one of the more significant paragraphs, Coppola explained his attitude toward money. "I am cavalier with money because it is necessary, so that I am not terrified each time I make an artistic decision. Do not confuse this attitude with the idea that I am tremendously rich. Many of you know that I am not. Remember one thing: the major companies and the distributors possess the one thing that is indispensable to the film director: the capital. My flamboyant refusal to obey such rules is also my greatest asset in dealing with them. It evens the stakes. . . ."

In 1977, Coppola was no longer forced to play the terrible Hollywood games. But he who had known the greatest success among the new Hollywood directors would soon encounter the first financial disaster of this "Hollywood Renaissance."

The reasons for it lie perhaps within his refusal to reconcile the contradictions of the commercial cinema with his own desire to produce more personal films, such as **The Rain People** or **The Conversation**, while still fighting Hollywood on its own turf with such blockbusters as **The Godfather, The Godfather, Part II**, or **Apocalypse Now**. It was as if, as a true artist, he was embarrassed at having too much money, the very sign of an artist not to be trusted.

It was a situation without resolution that left him unsatisfied with his personal films and somewhat embarrassed by the success of the others. At this point in his career, he did not know which way to turn. In interviews conducted at that time, Coppola often alluded to his father's failure as a musician. He equates this to the attitude of the screenwriter who believes that eighty percent of a film's success belongs to him. In Coppola's view, the director is merely the orchestra leader who combines the efforts of others. Hence his special feelings for **The Rain People** and **The Conversation**, the only two films over which he had complete control.

In spite of the enormous success of **The Godfather**, which brought him wealth, glory, and celebrity, Coppola was deeply affected by those in Hollywood who predicted that he would never again do anything as good. "I knew that it was impossible," he protests, "and anyway, it wasn't my intention."

For he had other projects in mind: "to make a film that was a moving human document, like a melody I heard once long ago and would like to recapture." He also expressed a preoccupation with the idea of making "modest films about contemporary human situations." But before returning to the cinema, he directed Noel Coward's *Private Lives* for the San Francisco American Conservatory.

He was also involved in the American premiere of Gottfried von Einem's *The Visit of the Old Lady* for the San Francisco Opera. He learned that "things get lost easily in opera and that music slows down the effects." He sees the medium of opera as "an artificial art form that needs to be stylized." The production received mixed reviews, and Coppola considered staging *Turandot*, a project which has since been indefinitely postponed.

The Great Gatsby

In one month, he wrote a faithful and sensitive adaptation of F. Scott Fitzgerald's novel *The Great Gatsby*, whose production had begun in 1971. At the time, Robert Evans, its producer, had wanted his current love interest, Ali McGraw, to play the role of Daisy, but Truman Capote's screenplay did not suit her.

Coppola was then called in to help. Jack Clayton, the director, remembers: "Francis performed a real miracle, just in time to pull us out of trouble . . . but he couldn't stay any longer to work on the screenplay because he was working on another film." **The Great Gatsby** wasn't completed until 1974, with a different cast. Coppola's adaptation was so comprehensive that one could think he read autobiographical implications into the story of Gatsby: the obscure beginnings followed by the great success. An illustration of the American Dream, in Fitzgerald's terms. Clayton would later claim that the few changes made to Coppola's version dealt with elements that were in the book. Coppola protested the elimination of two key scenes that were, in his eyes, essential to the film. The first was a long tête-à-tête sequence between Daisy and Jay Gatsby that took place in the bedroom. "An indispensable scene," claims Coppola, "to show that the lovers are together." Clayton cut the scene and dispersed parts of it throughout the second half of the film.

The other scene that was dear to Coppola showed the arrival of Gatsby's father after his son's murder. This scene reveals Gatsby's humble origins, which in turn explained his ambition. Central to this scene was a little notebook in which Jay, as a child, had written his plans for the future. Coppola's attraction to this detail was perhaps influenced by the fact that, as a child, he too had written such a note: "Dear Mom, I want to become rich and famous, but I am so discouraged. I don't think it will ever happen."

Like Jay Gatsby, Coppola was more concerned with the appearance of power than with its actual use.

Coppola and Clayton, through interviews, continued to blame each other for the film's eventual failure. Coppola went so far as to disclaim any role in the casting, and to claim that Clayton "overturned everything, the beginning, the middle, and the end, and made the film interminable."

After the film's release, Coppola declared: "I derive no pleasure from the process of directing. And *Gatsby* is a perfect example. If you had asked me, before *Gatsby*, whether I was a writer or a director, I would have answered that I was a writer who, from time to time, directed. But today, after what happened with *Gatsby*, I would give more credit to the director. He changed the screenplay and used the wrong lenses to shoot certain sequences, which ruined a good portion of the film."

His problems concerning this episode would soon be forgotten as he turned his attention to the 1974 Academy Awards: Robert De Niro won an Oscar for his interpretation of Vito Corleone in *The Godfather, Part II*. Carmine Coppola won an Oscar for the musical score, and Talia Shire, Francis's sister, was nominated for Best Supporting Actress. As the ultimate reward, *The Godfather, Part II* won the Oscar for Best Film of the year. Francis Coppola received the Oscar for Best Director, and shared Best Screenplay (adaptation) honors with Mario Puzo; also Dean Tavoularis received the award for Best Set Design (with Angelo Graham and George Nelson). *Gatsby* won an Oscar for Best Costumes.

The aging Godfather.

The secret listener: Gene Hackman in *The Conversation*.

5 The Ear That Sees

The Conversation

In the spring of 1973, after his theatrical interlude, Coppola turned his attention to a new original film project concerning an idea he had been toying with for nearly six years.

"I got the idea for *The Conversation* in 1967 or 1968, while listening to Irvin Kershner talk about espionage and surveillance tactics. Like Kubrick, Kershner was fascinated by all the latest state-of-the-art technology. He told me about microphones that were so powerful they could record a conversation between two people in the middle of a crowd. I was immediately struck by the idea, which seemed very visual and very cinematic, and I tried to build something around it." What he built was a scene between two people walking in a crowd whose conversation is interrupted each time someone walks in front of the microphone placed by another person. Coppola completed this first script in 1969 and already had Marlon Brando in mind. Coppola discussed the project with Brando, but nothing ever came of it. Over the next few months, Coppola modified the plot somewhat, by shifting the main interest from the "listenee" to the "listener." The first rumors about Watergate began surfacing just at the time when the film was going into production. But the rumors

concerning the severity of the scandal did not influence or change Coppola's project in any way. "At first, it did not seem very important. We were filming the warehouse scene then, and were two-thirds into the film. We heard about it but never suspected its actual meaning." For several years, Coppola had collected material of all kinds regarding clandestine listening practices, storing the details that could eventually be used for this film. "The political references in the film are slim, and were all contained in the first version. It seemed obvious to me that if such practices were being used in business, that they would naturally be used in politics, at election time for instance . . ."

Coppola admits to having been influenced by many different sources in writing the screenplay of *The Conversation*. Coppola, who does not bear an immeasurable admiration for Hitchcock, nevertheless recognized that "anyone who wants to direct a thriller inevitably becomes a student of Hitchcock's. After all, he created the genre." Coppola soon realized that "the only way to get the film financed was to set the intrigue on another level than that of Harry Caul's investigation. In my opinion, no one is going to go see a simple story of wiretapping. It had to be a kind of thriller, in the manner of Hitchcock's films. So I sat through all of his films to understand

why they worked so well."

He found Hitchcock's films to be "terribly overplayed." On the other hand, his admiration for Henri-Georges Clouzot was enormous, and he readily admits being influenced by his works: "I feel close to him because he goes beyond the thriller aspect in his films. He adds something more. I remember having seen *Diaboliques* in college, and I would like *The Conversation* to reproduce the same sort of effects." Another determining influence was that of Hermann Hesse. "I read *Steppenwolf* while I was writing *The Conversation* and I was very impressed by the character of Harry Haller. That is why the character in my film is also named Harry. He lives alone in an apartment as did the character in *Steppenwolf*."

Coppola had one other plan: to take advantage of this "personal" film to try some new techniques, specifically in the soundtrack. "I thought that Walter Murch might do the sound," explains Coppola. Murch was, like Lucas, a former USC student who had previously worked as a sound engineer on *The Rain People, THX 1138, American Graffiti,* and *The Godfather.* Coppola attached a great deal of importance to the soundtrack of a film. As Godard had advocated in the early 1970s, Coppola succeeded in "freeing the sound from the tyranny of the image." *The Conversation* is a film

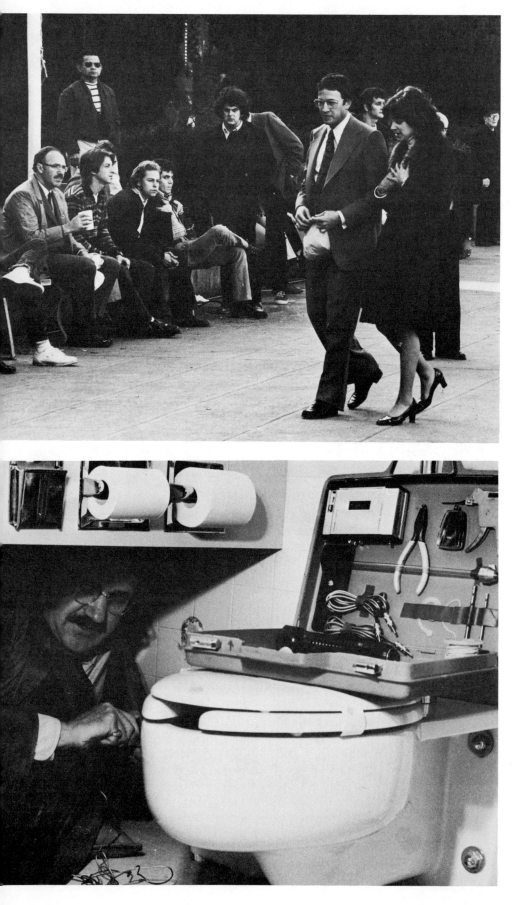

which must first be heard, then seen.

Professional Life and Private Life

The filming began at the end of 1972 and the film was presented in Cannes in 1974, while Coppola was finishing the location shots for *The Godfather, Part II* in Sicily. Gene Hackman played the leading role.

The Conversation's opening scene is a long shot of Union Square, a park in San Francisco. The camera moves and we hear a musical group playing "Red, Red Robin." A rapid zoom shot focuses on Harry Caul, a professional wiretapper and decipherer of coded messages. Harry, like Michael in *The Godfather* or Natalie in *The Rain People,* has a tragic flaw: Harry cannot draw the line between his private life and his professional life. Using the most sophisticated equipment, he is recording the conversation of a young couple in the park. Once the couple have left, Harry returns to his apartment. There he discovers, to his great surprise, as he thought he had the only key, that his superintendent has been inside the apartment.

The next day he goes to his office, which is located in an abandoned warehouse. He cuts and assembles the taped conversations of the couple.

That same evening he goes to visit Amy, a woman whom he occasionally helps financially. She begins to question him and he gets angry and walks out abruptly. Tense and irritated, Harry then refuses to hand over the tape to the assistant of "the Director," who has hired him for the job.

The man warns Harry not to get involved in the situation. But Harry returns to his office, where he tries to clarify one portion of the tape which had been difficult to hear. He finally gets a clear reading of the tape where the man is saying: "He'd kill us, if he got a chance."

Horrified by what he has heard, Harry goes to confession and tells the priest that his work will probably cause the death of two people. He nevertheless convinces himself that "he is not in any way responsible" for what may occur.

Harry attends a show on surveillance equipment, where he meets Bernie Moran. Moran believes that Harry is one of the top people in "the business." The assistant to the Director informs Harry that they are expecting the tape to be delivered on Sunday. Harry answers that he will think it over.

The same evening, Harry organizes a small get-together and invites Moran and Meredith, a prostitute with whom Harry makes love. That night, Harry dreams that he meets a woman and tells her stories of his past and of his childhood.

The next morning, Meredith and the tape have disappeared. He receives a telephone call and is told that the Director has an entire file on him. The assistant also tells him that the tape was taken in case he had any thoughts of destroying it, but that he could still pick up his money. In one of the taped conversations, the couple had spoken of a meeting arranged with the Director that was to take place in a hotel room that very day. Harry rents a room in the same hotel, right next door to the room where the meeting is to take place, and installs his equipment. When he hears the noise of a struggle in the adjoining room, he hides under the covers, but when the noise subsides, he goes into the next room, using his pass-key. Everything seems in order. Instinctively, he flushes the toilet, and blood rushes onto the carpet. Harry rushes to the Director's office, but changes his mind at the last minute. Walking by a newsstand, he reads the headline on the newspaper: the Director has been killed in an automobile accident.

He soon realizes that he misinterpreted what he heard on the tape. He thought the couple was afraid of being killed by the Director, whereas it was the couple who intended to kill the Director.

Harry returns to his apartment,

where another telephone call informs him that he now knows too much and will therefore be placed under surveillance. He frantically searches his apartment for hidden wires but cannot find any. Discouraged, he gives up and, sitting in the middle of his empty apartment, begins playing the saxophone . . .

The Death of Clandestinity

The film was well received by the American critics, but the audiences did not follow suit. In spite of the Palme d'Or it received in Cannes, *The Conversation* was not a financial success.

Stanley Kauffmann described *The Conversation* as "an interesting and satisfying film, handling a serious subject with extraordinary cinematographic skill." Others applauded "Coppola's first film revealing his social conscience and intellectual honesty." "Never have the walls had so many ears. Never have objects spied on us with such intensity," wrote Jean-Louis Bory. "This represents the end of secrecy, the end of clandestinity. But secrecy is the only refuge of the average man. Only there can he free himself of all pressure and conditioning. If secrecy has become impossible, so has liberty. That is what Coppola is saying. . . . It is no longer the eye that hears, but the ear that sees. And Coppola has chosen a simple story with ordinary people. That is his way of showing that anyone can be watched and monitored. . . . Coppola shrewdly uses the banality of this story, for it is no longer protective, it no longer protects us. We are more sensitized to the fact that fear is born of our suddenly revealed insecurity."

Coppola claimed to have made a film "not about intimacy," as he had originally planned, "but about responsibility," as he had done in *The Rain People*.

This film showed unquestionable

The unraveling hero of *The Conversation*.

Opposite page, top: **Gene Hackman, lost in the crowd. In the foreground, Frederic Forrest and Cindy Williams.**

Opposite page, bottom: **Gene Hackman, alone against the world.**

45

Surveillance in Union Square.

and remarkable technical genius. To listen first, and then to see . . .

This film also described, without ever offering a solution, the destruction of intimacy, in such a way as to make us shudder. What is our responsibility? Are we all destined to live like rats? As Coppola began to understand the subject's political implications, he realized that one has to work with the public, on a political scale. He admitted this, saying he had watched "many films by Frank Capra." But if Capra's heroes were often naïve, they were nevertheless very active. If Coppola were to make *The Conversation* again, he would probably not have Harry Caul as the film's center of interest.

The Elusive Power

According to Coppola, Gene Hackman had read the script before the success of *The French Connection*. But after the success of *The French Connection,* Hackman served as a financial guarantee for Coppola's project. Coppola also described how Hackman arrived on the set suntanned and had to be transformed into the pallid, sallow, graying, bespectacled Harry Caul.

In spite of Gene Hackman's irreproachable performance in what was a most difficult role, it was hard for the film's main character to sustain the audience's attention for two straight hours. Harry Caul is a complex being who falls apart little by little throughout the film.

Coppola agrees that he undertook an arduous if not impossible task: "It was very difficult to come to terms with a principal character who, during the entire length of the film, never speaks to or confides in anyone."

To those who criticized him for having presented the two other characters through a recorded conversation (an experiment in itself), Coppola replies that too often "films look alike because they are always made in the same way, and because the public wants it that way. Films are too expensive to produce to be used experimentally. In those cases, one has to be rich and able to finance one's films independently."

Concerning that particular sequence, Coppola adds: "I tried, deliberately, not to present the characters in the traditional manner. I wanted to 'suggest' them. It was my way of trying to find a different way to present a character to the audience." Pacino had once remarked about Coppola: "Francis is an emotional voyeur. He looks, he sees, he observes the emotions of others. He cannot help himself."

Much of the credit for the film goes to Walter Murch, who was not only responsible for the soundtrack but who also cut the film.

As is his habit, Coppola had filmed several takes of each scene and had even filmed alternate versions of certain sequences. Murch was the one to sort through the mountains of film to give a logical progression to the story. By this time, Coppola was already involved in filming *The Godfather, Part II. The Rain People* and *The Conversation,* Coppola's only films based on his original screenplays, were both conceived without a definite end. Coppola is afraid of the written word. Yet, during all of his interviews, he always expresses his strong desire to be a writer.

If his writing abilities are not yet obvious to all, no one can question his screenwriting ability. Thanks to this talent, Coppola gave new life to a genre that used to depend on reference—the thriller. As Coppola redefines it, the thriller has nothing to do with nostalgia. Alan J. Pakula's *Klute* had already foreshadowed this renewed genre.

The anonymity which haunts individuals can swallow them up at any moment. Coppola's stroke of genius was to have shifted this concrete magnetism to the very writing of the film. For once, repression was found where it belongs, i.e., in the nerve center. A man's elusive power, as intermediary between the others, is destroyed and he is rendered defenseless when he himself is the victim of this insidious penetration.

Coppola had wanted to give his film "a moral and humanistic conclusion." "*The Conversation* ends with an image of madness, a madness that threatens the contemporary world, if it does not safeguard itself against the progress of technology," wrote Jean-Loup Passek. Never have the walls had so many ears . . .

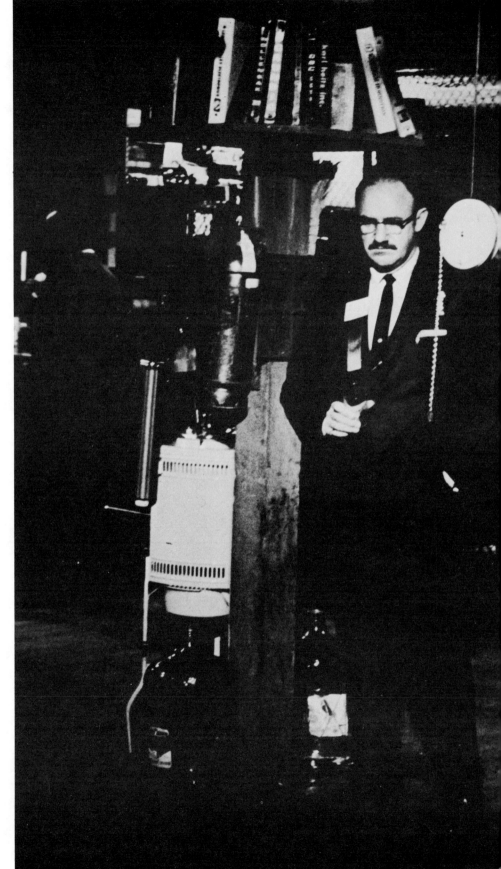

A confused Gene Hackman in *The Conversation*.

Young Vito Corleone (Robert De Niro), about to conquer the New World in *The Godfather, Part II*.

6 Final Payments

The Godfather, Part II

"The very thought of devising a sequel to *The Godfather* was unbearable to me," Coppola confesses when asked about his role in the creation of the second part of the Corleone family saga. "It would have smacked of opportunism and I had once said, as a joke, that the only way I would agree to do it was if I could do *Abbott and Costello Meet the Godfather* . . ."

On a more serious note, Coppola admitted that, given the amount of money he had earned with *The Godfather,* the only reason for which he might agree to direct its sequel was because "he wanted to."

Coppola knew that a screenplay entitled *The Death of Michael Corleone* had already been submitted to Paramount. Turning his attention to the project, he felt that the public had not morally condemned the character of Michael at the end of *The Godfather.* This would give him a lead into the next episode: "I wanted to take Michael toward what was, in fact, his destiny, and the film's logical conclusion. After winning all the battles and overcoming all of his enemies, thanks to his intelligence and superiority, I did not want to see him die. Nor did I want him to go to jail. Or be assassinated by his rivals. But, in a larger

sense, I wanted him to be a broken man. And there is no doubt, in the last scene of the film, that Michael, sitting in the chair, victorious but alone, is a living corpse." Coppola wanted Michael to be a "condemned man, for he is someone who would never change. I did toy with the idea of having a sudden turnabout at the end, where Michael might turn against his father and refuse to take over his role, but honesty—and Pacino—prevented me from going any further."

Coppola informed Paramount of his decision to go ahead with the project, but only on the condition that he be allowed to use the actors of his choice. He also demanded total control over the film's production.

This time, Coppola wrote the screenplay on his own, but Mario Puzo did eventually make some contributions to the script. The first version was not acceptable to Pacino. So, according to Maureen Orth, "Coppola rewrote the entire thing in three days, and the scripts were photostated barely in time for the first rehearsal." After the first reading, the actors all stood and applauded Coppola.

Coppola had wished to have Marlon Brando once again, but the relationship between the actor and Paramount was rather cool. Coppola soon realized he had better not count on Brando's presence in this sequel. Although he was disappointed at first, "after

having worked with Robert De Niro, it was clear that he could easily play a young Vito (younger than Marlon Brando), and that was what I wanted." Coppola also developed Kay's role, and showed the problems growing in the marriage. "They have been together for six or seven years. How many husbands swear to their wives that things will be better as soon as they close a good deal or as soon as they make a hundred thousand dollars? Even I have repeatedly sworn to my wife, during our thirteen years of marriage, that I would not work as hard or that I would stop altogether. It's a classic situation. And if Michael lies to Kay in such a way that she believes him, it is because she is prepared to believe him."

This production reinforced Coppola's views on his role in the film business: "People like me who agree to work within the system—but who are capable of changing it or of becoming independent enough to finance their own work—people like me will be unquestionably taken in by the system if they ever compromise with it." To illustrate his point, he refers to several "young, talented authors and directors who are very successful in Hollywood. I had even offered some of them jobs, four or five years back. Today, they make a great deal of money, but they have changed. They are strictly concerned with business, with new

49

markets. They swoon over their cars and their houses that have cost them half a million dollars. And without realizing it, they have become the very people they used to criticize. . . . That is one of the reasons why I choose to live in San Francisco and not in Los Angeles. I try to keep a certain distance and to maintain a sense of reality."

One Wrong Move and You're Dead

The projected budget for *The Godfather, Part II* was substantial, and Coppola realized that the film would have to gross at least twenty-five million dollars just to break even.

Hence the following description he offered of his job at the time: "Being a director is like running in front of a train. If you stop, or you trip, you're dead. How can you have any imagination with something like that behind you? The workdays cost eight thousand dollars per hour. That helps you to make efficient decisions!"

The filming began on October 1, 1973, at Lake Tahoe, with the scene of Anthony's communion, followed by the outdoor scenes in New York and Las Vegas. The Italian sequenes were filmed in June of 1974. The following January, as they were shooting in Santo Domingo, it rained every day. Al Pacino's health became a concern to all: "The role of Michael was a very strange and difficult one, and caused Al a great deal of stress," says Coppola. "In *The Godfather,* his character evolved during the course of the film, from a young, naïve, and brilliant student to a cold and determined killer. In *The Godfather, Part II,* he is the same man from beginning to end. Al had to function on the same key, in a very subtle manner, throughout the film. He is constantly walking the fine edge without one chance of letting himself go. His entire performance is an understatement, and it is impossible for Pacino to know whether he is creating

a monster or playing a 'bad guy.' Pacino's responsibility was enormous and had completely exhausted him."

Nine months later, the shooting had been completed within the anticipated schedule. Because the film was too long, all the scenes concerning the young Vito Corleone had to be eliminated. "My heart was really in those sequences shot in Little Italy, in the old streets of New York that were filled with music and the atmosphere of the turn of the century," said Coppola regretfully. "I had other beautiful scenes in mind that I was never able to include in the film. In one of them, Caruso was seen singing 'Over There,' a patriotic song of World War I that encouraged young men to enlist. Others included Italian construction workers building the New York subway, and Vito Corleone courting his fiancée and joining his friends for a drink."

The worldwide preview was planned for Christmas of 1974, but during a sneak preview in San Diego, Coppola noticed a problem in the editing. *Time* magazine noticed it too and promptly reported to its readers that the last scene was confusing and cold, that other sequences were too long or should have been eliminated altogether. During the screening, Coppola dictated notes to himself into a tape recorder. Once he had returned to San Francisco, he completed the final cut in a few days, an effort that led him to say that "never again would [he] work under such conditions," adding that, given three additional months, he could have made a "great film."

The First Break

Two stories alternate within the film. The first one begins with a close-up shot of Michael's face. Then, a slow funeral procession: young Vito's father, who was killed for standing up to the Mafia in his Sicilian village, is being buried. On the way to the cemetery, noises are heard: Vito's mother

and brother will also be shot. Vito escapes and reaches the United States, arriving at Ellis Island.

The film jumps to the present with the scene of Michael's eldest son's communion. Senator Geary refuses to grant Michael a gambling license and Jimmy Ola, Roth's man, tries to set up a meeting between his boss and Michael.

Michael's sister Connie announces that she wants to marry again. Frankie Pentangeli warns Michael that Roth's men intend to harm him. But Michael does not react. Later, Kay tells Michael that she is pregnant and reproaches him for not having kept his promise to abandon his activities. That same night, there is an assassination attempt made on him.

Flashback to young Vito in 1917, after his marriage to Carmella. The young couple live in a modest apartment and Vito works in a grocery store in Little Italy, owned by Signor Abbandando. Abbandando's son takes Vito to the opera, where Vito first sees the famous Fanucci, the local boss of the Black Hand. Fanucci is extorting money from the theater's director by threatening to kill his daughter, Carla. A few days later, Fanucci asks Abbandando to give Fanucci's nephew a job in his store. Vito is soon fired. During this time, Vito meets Clemenza, a small-time gangster who once asked Vito to hide some firearms for him. In return for this favor, Clemenza gives Vito a stolen rug.

Back to the present. Michael is in Miami, with Hyman Roth, in Roth's bungalow. Michael tells Roth of his decision to eliminate Frankie, who planned the assassination attempt. Then Michael visits Frankie and asks for his help: Michael tells Frankie that Roth is behind the murder attempt, and Michael wants Frankie to find out who Roth's accomplice was. Meanwhile, Freddie Corleone receives a telephone call from Johnny Ola, who asks him for another favor. During a meeting between Rosato and Frankie, two men try to strangle Frankie, tell-

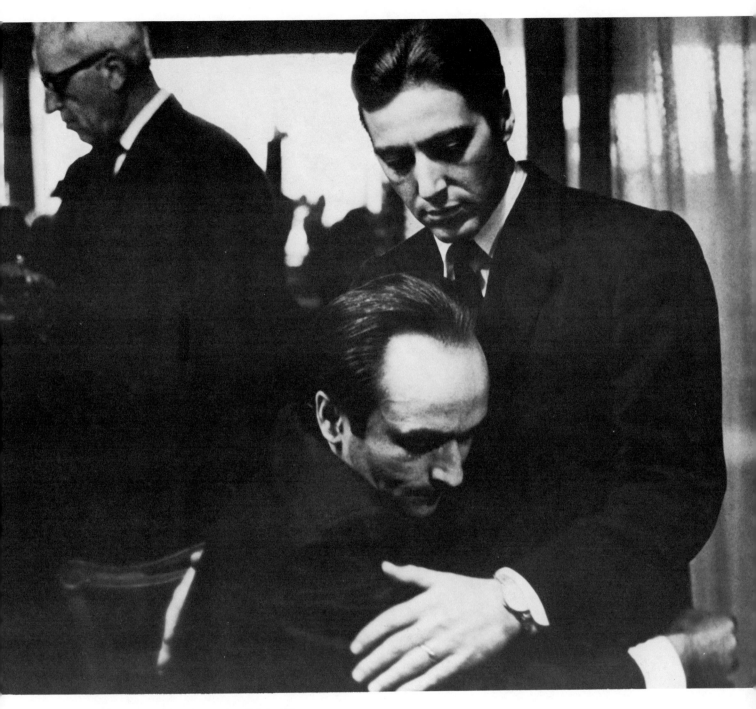

John Cazale asks his brother (Al Pacino) to forgive him.

The portrait of a family. John Cazale, James Gounaris, Al Pacino, and Diane Keaton.

ing him "this is from Michael." His life is saved by the unexpected arrival of a policeman. In a Las Vegas brothel, Senator Geary wakes up next to a dead prostitute. In exchange for Michael's help, Geary will grant him the gambling license.

In Havana, the representatives of the American authorities are warmly received by the Cuban president, who is also on good terms with Hyman Roth. Hyman Roth and Michael are both present at the celebration, where Michael has offered a "gift" of two million dollars to the dictator. When the unrest begins, Michael is concerned and hesitates, but Hyman threatens him by saying that if the money does not arrive within the next few hours, their deal will be off.

As soon as Freddie arrives with the money, Michael decides to eliminate Roth, who, Michael suspects, is planning another attempt on his life. Michael's bodyguard kills Johnny Ola, but is then murdered himself, just as he was about to kill Roth in a hospital room. During the evening, the Cuban president resigns. The news causes panic among the guests. Michael is able to escape, but cannot convince Freddie to return to Las Vegas with him. Michael now knows that Freddie was Roth's accomplice. The Cuban operation is a total fiasco.

Upon his return, Michael learns that Kay has had a miscarriage.

Back in New York, Vito is now working for a tailor. He has formed a gang with his friends Tessio and Clemenza. When Fanucci learns of its existence, he demands money from them. Vito kills Fanucci during a religious ceremony.

There follows a long sequence that traces Michael's investigation by a Senate committee. Cicci, one of the witnesses, agrees to name names as he has done several "jobs" for the Corleone family. But nothing can implicate Michael, who is growing increasingly concerned about his problems with Kay.

Michael begins asking his mother questions about his past, trying to un-

derstand the true nature and personality of his father. What made Vito Corleone a success was his ability to preserve the unity of the family, this same family that is progressively falling apart.

Vito gains the trust of the local merchants, who are grateful for Fanucci's disappearance. A friend of Vito's wife, Signora Colombo, asks Vito for his help in preventing her landlord from evicting her. Vito settles the problem as his import-export company grows: the future seems promising . . .

Michael appears before the committee. He denies having assassinated a policeman and having organized the executions of the heads of the five New York families. But the committee has a witness named Frankie Pentangeli. Afraid for his life, Frankie has placed himself under the protection of the FBI and has made specific accusations against the Corleone family. When he suddenly spots his brother Vincenzo in the audience, sitting next to Michael, Pentangeli withdraws his accusations.

Kay is humiliated by the scandal and announces her decision to take the children and leave Michael. When he refuses, she tells him that the miscarriage was actually an abortion. Disgusted, he throws her out, but keeps the children.

In another flashback, Vito, who has returned to Sicily for a visit, stabs the old leader of the local Mafia who had killed his parents and his older brother.

In Lake Tahoe, Michael, Freddie, and Connie are together for the burial of their mother. Connie decides to remain there and look after Michael. She asks him to forgive Freddie and let him return to the family compound.

Inflexible as ever, Michael has Freddie killed during a fishing trip. He also has Roth killed in Miami. A different flashback this time takes us to 1942, following the Japanese attack on Pearl Harbor. Michael had joined the Marines, taken his life in his own hands rather than follow the rules of the family. It had been his first gesture of

independence, his first break with the family.

The film ends with two rapid sequences: Vito leaving Sicily forever, and Michael, sitting alone in his immense Lake Tahoe compound.

The Sicilian Waltz of Vengeance

"I wanted to show how two men, a father and a son, could be corrupted by this Sicilian waltz of vengeance," said Coppola, talking about *The Godfather, Part II*. Mainly, the film concerns themes that were merely outlined in *The Godfather*, but it does so in a more intellectual and less frenetic manner. Coppola's screenplay carries the plot well beyond the limits of Puzo's book.

The audience's reaction to *The Godfather* had been excellent, and for good reason. The film was a masterpiece of its genre, but that alone could not account for the success of both the book and film. It had to do with the basis upon which Coppola and Puzo created their works. None of the preceding films on the Mafia had even been remotely as successful as *The Godfather*. What Puzo understood—and what Coppola developed—was that the main attraction stemmed from the family aspect of the film. *The Godfather*'s main strength was contained in its title: it was the story of a father and of a son.

It told the story of a generation of immigrants for whom the streets of America were paved with gold. The victims fully understood the choices made by the Corleone family and no one would question their power. What was also accepted, in this film, was the fact that this was the only way for the Corleone family to succeed, to reach "the American dream." If Vito became rich, it was necessarily at the expense of others. And if his way of settling things was a violent one, its violence was considerably lessened when taken in the context of the time in question. *The Godfather* looked like an "action" film, but actually it was a film about relationships and influences between men and women, and between men and their sons. Vito's ultimate tragedy was that he had to separate his business and private lives; Michael's was that he could not.

A film such as *The Godfather*, which opens with a long wedding sequence and offers other such family scenes, cannot be seen as a "gangster movie."

The Godfather, Part II deals with the same themes, but in a more profound way. The part of the film that concerned Vito's early days had been cut from *The Godfather* due to the film's length, but its reappearance in *The Godfather, Part II* helps to explain the choices and decisions made by Vito, as he grew older.

The second film is mainly about Michael, and, by extension, about Kay. She is a prisoner of her marriage, and as such she is reminescent of Natalie in *The Rain People*, who was, like many women, metaphorically sequestered.

The Godfather, Part II also draws parallels between the family business and business in general. What is good for the family is also good for America. As Michael had said to the senator: "We are both part of the same hypocrisy." Coppola may be identifying with Michael at such moments: both had started out filled with ideals and both would eventually be caught up in a web of traditions forcing them to do the things they had once found contemptible.

Coppola gave Roger Corman and other Hollywood personalities parts in the film (the roles of senators), and Lee Strasberg played Hyman Roth.

From a cinematographic point of view, the film was brilliant. Gordon Willis, the director of photography, captured the crude light of southern Italy as precisely as he did the sepia tones of America in the 1940s. "The direction was classic," said *Positif*. "The luxurious sets are always secondary to a specific gesture or a point that is being discussed. There are few camera movements, few traveling shots other than those that follow the main character—Vito—as he arrives in Ellis Island, or Fanucci covering his territory in Little Italy, and they serve to mirror the characters' impressions: fear, curiosity, vanity.

"Coppola captures his characters in their most revealing and fitting gestures. . . . His classical and serene composition, his steady and measured direction of the actors, give the film a sense of paradoxical confidence, similar to the violent lucidity of the pessimistic closing sequence." Frédéric Vitoux concludes: "One senses that Coppola does not despair in his chosen work, or in America, given the clarity of expression he attains without covering up what today's system condemns."

The Godfather, Part II earned thirty million dollars in the United States, quite an achievement for a film that combines two separate stories, one-third of which is in Italian with English subtitles.

One of the reasons for the film's success was undoubtedly the affection and warmth Coppola used in depicting the details that so powerfully evoked the 1940s and 1950s. The film dissected one of the myths of the American Dream by revealing the inherent dilemmas facing all the immigrants who knew themselves to be "all undesirables." How many immigrants had come across men like Vito?

Coppola recreated this moment in time for the millions of Americans who would no longer be ashamed of their past. By doing so, he made of *The Godfather, Part II* a film as important as *Citizen Kane*. Charles Foster Kane and Vito Andolini Corleone were like brothers. Both could explain America's mentality better than any history book.

After the film's release, Coppola decided to concentrate on more personal projects. "I am almost thirty-five years old; this is the end of the first part of my life and the best time to take stock and decide what changes I want to make."

The Godfather earned Coppola more money than he had ever hoped, and gave him the means of making "his own modest film," *The Conversation* (as well as his theater productions). Now he intended to turn to writing, to experiment with comedy. "My definition of success used to be to wake up, go for a walk and see something that obsessed you, then return home and write a screenplay that you would eventually direct. According to my own definition, then, I have succeeded."

Starting November 12, 1977, and for the next three evenings, NBC broadcast *The Godfather Saga*, a complete novel for television. Coppola, who was already involved in *Apocalypse Now*, had left the responsibility of the new editing to Barry Malkin. It ran over nine hours, but was not as successful as the cinema version.

The second generation: the new Godfather, Al Pacino.

"This is the end." Martin Sheen in *Apocalypse Now*.

7 In the Heart of Darkness

Apocalypse Now

The filming of *Apocalypse Now* has become part of the history of the cinema, alongside such legendary productions as *The Birth of a Nation, Gone with the Wind,* and *Cleopatra*.

Millions of dollars went up in smoke, and were carried away by torrential rains, during this titanic undertaking.

The project was first brought to Coppola's attention while he was filming *The Rain People* in 1969. He knew very little of war, as he readily admits, but John Milius had told him many stories about Vietnam. When Milius and George Lucas asked Coppola for his help in preparing a film based on these stories, Coppola suggested they use Joseph Conrad's *Heart of Darkness* as a basis, using the metaphor of the boat and constructing the plot around a mysterious Colonel Kurtz. (In the book, Charlie Marlow, a sailor, tells of his journey along an African river in search of Mr. Kurtz, who represents a European trading company.)

Warner Bros. offered John Milius fifteen thousand dollars to write a first draft. In six weeks, Lucas and Milius had written *Apocalypse Now*. Coppola describes it as "a comedy and a terrifying psychological horror story." What happened next has already been mentioned: Warner Bros. cancelled all of its forthcoming projects with American Zoetrope (including *Apocalypse Now* and *The Conversation*), forcing Coppola to buy back the scripts at a cost of four hundred thousand dollars. Coppola intended nevertheless to produce this film, for he liked its subject. But by then, John Milius was involved in writing *The Life and Times of Judge Roy Bean* (directed by John Huston) and Lucas was preparing *Star Wars*. Coppola decided, on the spur of the moment, to do the film himself. "I thought that it would be fun to take a good screenplay, set up a good distribution system, and make a film without having to go through all of the anguish and horrors I had suffered during the production of both *Godfather*s."

The initial project—a documentary-style film to be shot in 16-millimeter and budgeted at a cost of one and a half million dollars—was abandoned.

"From 1975 on, the enormous plans for *Apocalypse Now* both nourished and threatened the survival of Zoetrope," says Jack Fritz, one of the company's executives.

The Oscars Go out the Window

In November of 1975, Coppola, with John Milius's screenplay in hand, began contacting the actors he wanted for his film.

Steve McQueen thought the role of Willard was an excellent one, but not for him. Coppola offered to rewrite the part in collaboration with McQueen. McQueen accepted, liked the revised script, but could not leave the United States.

At first, Marlon Brando would not answer Coppola's telephone calls. Brando's agent told Coppola he was not interested in the film. Coppola then sent a copy of the screenplay to Al Pacino, who, remembering the miseries of shooting on location in Santo Domingo, could not bear the thought of a seventeen-week stay in the jungle. Coppola then offered the role of Kurtz to Steve McQueen, with a promise of no more than three weeks of shooting. But the actor still demanded three million dollars, the same amount he had asked for seventeen weeks of shooting.

Coppola then offered the role of Willard to James Caan for one million two hundred and fifty thousand dollars, but Caan wanted two million. When Coppola began pressuring him, Caan admitted that his wife was pregnant and refused to give birth in the Philippines.

Coppola considered Jack Nicholson, but nothing came of it. Robert Redford thought the role of Willard was interesting, but nevertheless declined, having promised his family he would not go anywhere on location for the remainder of the year.

Eleonor Coppola filming the unreleased documentary about *Apocalypse Now*.

Coppola withdrew his previous offer of the role of Kurtz to Steve McQueen and turned to Nicholson, who declined.

When Coppola failed to convince Pacino to play the part of Kurtz, he threw his Oscars out the window. Four of the five shattered and his children picked up the pieces.

Finally, Brando agreed to meet with Coppola.

Backed by the three prestigious names of Marlon Brando, Steve McQueen, and Gene Hackman, Coppola had obtained eight million dollars in financing for American Zoetrope from foreign distributors (Japan having contributed one million dollars). Of the three actors, only Brando was signed, at a price of two million dollars for five weeks of shooting.

Coppola proposed the following choice to his investors: either a full reimbursement, or a thirty-percent refund. All chose the second alternative. United Artists, who would distribute the film in the United States and in Canada, contributed an additional $7,000,000 to the remaining $6,400,000.

Despite these initial mishaps, the project was still financially sound. A budget of fourteen million dollars afforded Coppola full control over the film while making him solely responsible for any budget overruns.

Apocalypse When?

On March 1, 1976, the entire Coppola family, including Francis's wife, chil-

dren, nephews, baby-sitter, and private projectionist, left for the Philippines, a location chosen for its resemblance to Vietnam. The film crew's ability to rent helicopters "made in the U.S.A." and the low cost of labor made it a good location choice.

Four hundred and fifty technicians had already built a set and prepared the actors' wardrobe.

On March 20, Coppola shot the first scene, Willard's helicopter trip, bringing him to the start of his mission.

On April 2, during the rehearsal of an intricate action scene, the helicopters, which were being piloted by Filipinos, were suddenly called to the south of the country to fight the rebels.

On April 8, Francis Coppola celebrated his thirty-seventh birthday with hamburgers and hot dogs specially flown in from San Francisco.

The first rushes, back from Rome (along with a supply of pasta and olive oil), were viewed on April 16. The scenes with Harvey Keitel, as Captain Willard, caused general consternation. Coppola decided to catch the first plane back to Los Angeles. Having shaved his beard, lost weight, and exchanged his glasses for contact lenses, Coppola was unrecognizable. He had fired Keitel, who was performing "too feverishly, like background actors who try to catch the viewers' attention." Within minutes, Coppola hired a little-known actor, Martin Sheen, who began his part on April 24.

Around this time, Coppola began having difficulties with the parts of the screenplay that concerned Willard's journey. Also, "there were increasing similarities between Kurtz and Francis," recalls Eleonor Coppola in the journal she kept during the filming and which was eventually published as *Notes*.

On May 15, the last location shot at Baler was completed: it involved an air attack led by Robert Duvall. To simulate a napalm bombardment, five thousand liters of gasoline were burned in ninety seconds.

On May 26, following eight straight days of torrential rain, a typhoon destroyed the main set at Iba, on the river. Coppola decided to make use of this unfortunate accident by returning to the United States while a new set was being built further up the river. Coppola rewrote the screenplay but could not find a suitable ending. "I wrote so many grandiose endings . . . like that of *The Bridge on the River Kwai,* but I kept saying to myself: not like that, it's too much like a movie, and what I am doing is 'not like a movie.' "

Eleonor Coppola recounts that "the typhoon gave him an excuse to stop everything and try and solve his problems. Until that point, he had not dared to, knowing that too much money had been spent. At the same

Top: **Francis Coppola and Fred Roos, the producer, in the Philippines in 1977, on location for** *Apocalypse Now.*

Bottom: **The director standing in front of the Playboy bunnies' helicopter.**

Top: **Aurore Clément in the French plantation sequence that was cut from the film's final version.**

Bottom: **Coppola and Duvall in Lieutenant Colonel Kilgore's helicopter.**

time, he was discouraged at the thought of not being able to adapt his personal vision."

On August 3, the famous opening sequence in the hotel room was filmed with Martin Sheen in the role of Willard. After being locked in his room for two straight days, Willard is in an "altered" state. Coppola had set up two cameras and let Sheen play himself to the limit. When Sheen accidentally cut himself by hitting a mirror, Coppola wanted to cut. But Sheen insisted that they go on, and they did. Sheen later admitted that he would not look at the rushes of that particular scene and didn't see any of it until it was in its final form.

On August 8, the crew was shooting the Do Long bridge sequence where the Vietcong were to blow up a bridge measuring forty-five meters. More than five hundred smoke bombs, one hundred sticks of phosphorus dynamite, five thousand liters of gasoline, thirty-five sticks of dynamite for each of the fifty water explosions, two thousand rockets, torches, and tracer shells, and no less than ten miles of Bickford cord were needed to set up the shot, which lasted only ninety seconds.

But the scene in question had to be shot over and over again, and each additional day of filming cost between $30,000 and $35,000. Aurore Clément and Christian Marquand arrived from France to shoot the scenes that were to take place on the French plantation. Willard and his men arrive at the abandoned plantation where a hostile French couple had been hiding out for some time. Willard and his team are at first wary of them, then demand ammunition, rape the woman, and kill the man before resuming their journey. Coppola changed the scene to give it a more political tone, including a long discussion about the former French position in Southeast Asia, and the loss of Dien Bien Phu. In the final cut, Coppola left out this entire sequence. He also had another problem to contend with: Marlon Brando's weight. Brando refused to shoot a scene in which his weight was actually written into the script.

Coppola and Brando discussed the part for weeks. Coppola explained that there were two images of Kurtz in Conrad's book: "The first shows a skull that looks as if it were made of ivory, the second, that of a man hidden in the shadows. We chose to do a stylized interpretation. Brando/Kurtz would be lying the the dark. It was a film about good and evil, and he was mad. We wanted a character that was oversized, theatrical, larger than life. After the long journey on the river, the film would not tolerate any classic action scenes. It was not a time for intrigues, but a time for ideas, for an experience and a transformation to occur between Willard and Kurtz. For two months, the film had taken a mystical turn and I was becoming a kind of guru."

By October 8, the scenes with Brando were completed and the actor left the set.

The Coppola family returned to San Francisco for the year-end holidays.

The year 1977 started off badly, with the news of Martin Sheen's heart attack on March 5. Eleonor would remark at a later date that "Francis himself was making the film's journey; he was looking for himself and perhaps that was what scared him the most. For at the journey's end, he would be confronted with another him, which explained his inability to find an adequate ending for the film. He was afraid of failure, of death and of going mad."

On April 1, the crew celebrated the two-hundredth day of shooting with fireworks that spelled out APOCALYPSE NOW, 200TH, GOOD LUCK FRANCIS.

Martin Sheen returned to the set on April 19.

Finally, on May 21, 1977, Coppola thanked the crew with the traditional wrap speech. He declared that never in his life had he seen "so many people happy to be out of a job."

Coppola with Dennis Hopper as the photographer.

His Filmic Opera

Coppola flew to Europe to view the rushes with his team of editors and the Italian crew.

In July, Coppola was still in debt for fifteen million dollars in cost overruns. But his anguish was just beginning. The editing and mixing took forever.

Despite its increasing exasperation, United Artists agreed to delay the projected opening date from May to October 1977. Coppola was having marital difficulties and could not finish the film. He was still dissatisfied and worked day and night, vacillating between exhilaration and devastation, ready to start all over again, questioning his talent, then marveling at his own genius . . .

He added certain sequences filmed on his estate in Napa Valley, near San Francisco, where he had arranged to have certain sets brought back from the Philippines! He improved the film's soundtrack, and had Michael Herr write Willard's voice-over monologue.

On April 23, 1978, nine hundred people saw the first complete sneak preview of the definitive version of *Apocalypse Now.*

After the screening, Coppola drew up a list of his problems and of the film's problems, as if the two were connected. "What are my problems?"

he asked himself. "My greatest fear concerns the film's weak points: the narration and the style. More importantly, the end does not work either from the public's point of view or from a philosophical viewpoint. Then, the audience is disappointed in Brando and the film reaches its impact point during that damn helicopter attack."

A Work in Progress

In October of 1978, Coppola decided definitely to cut out the French plantation sequence which, he says, "never really fit into the story." Thousands of dollars' worth of film were thus locked up in a tin can and placed on a shelf to collect dust.

Then Coppola had a sudden illumination concerning the presentation of what he would eventually refer to as his "filmic opera." The viewers would be seated in total darkness. The only sounds to be heard were those of the jungle. Then came the opening sequence. The film would end with the image of the boat and the river diminishing and eventually fading into darkness. The credits would roll only once the theater lights were back on. But that version would never be shown.

A second opening date, Christmas Day 1979, was also postponed. Coppola was traveling throughout the country, organizing several sneak previews of the film. He then planned an "audience reaction" screening with his friends and employees from the

Bay Area, followed by a second one in Westwood. A third such screening was given for President Carter at the White House.

The film was finally presented to the rest of the world at the Cannes Film Festival. Coppola expressly demanded that the film be labeled "in progress," but that it not be excluded from the competition, for, as he said "from the moment you present a film, you are in competition."

In the version that was presented at Cannes, Willard kills Kurtz, refuses to get back on the boat, and thus remains in the lair. "An ending that was my ending," insists Coppola. "But the audience never liked it. Nor did the people in my company. I think the ending of my film was a lie, because I believe that the Vietnam war was a pack of lies. That is why I thought the ending was fitting."

In the 70-millimeter version, Willard leaves Kurtz's kingdom but does not give the order, over the radio, to "terminate his subjects."

Apocalypse Now would win, along with Volker Schlöndorff's *The Tin Drum*, the Palme d'Or of the Thirty-second International Film Festival at Cannes.

A Season in Hell

"This is the end." A man is dreaming and his nightmare fills the screen. Images of war telescope his dizziness. He has not avoided the horror: there follows a sensorial spin into the immediate terror of war. A relentless pounding of disturbing sensations that are like a psychedelic trip, anticipating the voyage to come. The other voyage.

The man's voice comes from an indistinct future: "I was going to the worst place in the world, but I didn't even know it yet. Weeks away and hundred of miles up a river that snaked through the war like a main circuit cable plugged straight into Kurtz."

The man who is speaking is Captain Benjamin Willard, the man who handles the impossible missions.

Marlon Brando, Coppola, and Martin Sheen preparing the final scene.

Saigon . . .

This time, the mission is "more like a penance." It begins with a trip up the river through Cambodia and ends with the execution of Kurtz, who has built a kingdom of sorts for himself, where he massacres and philosophizes at will.

"It was no accident that I got to be the caretaker of Colonel Walter E. Kurtz's memory," says the voice-over, "any more than being back in Saigon was an accident. There is no way to tell his story without telling mine, and if his story is really a confession, then so is mine."

The journey begins. "Fasten your seat belts, it's going to be a bumpy night." The men who form the crew aboard the boat that will take Willard toward his secret goal are all symbols, symbolic Americans who, except for the black captain, wish only to return home and resume their previous lives (surfing, cooking, and rock and roll). But for Willard, there may be no return. "Trouble is," says the voice, "I'd been back there and I knew that it just didn't exist anymore . . ." What would have vanished, according to Willard, was the very idea of a secure and stable America. Ironically, Coppola makes a parallel comment concerning the film director's attitude toward a world that, outside of Vietnam, no longer exists. That is why the

Martin Sheen taking a break.

63

The attack on a Vietcong village.

strangeness of Vietnam is purposely repressed in favor of the film's desire to show how Americans can reproduce their own "facsimile" of home wherever they go. Willard's meeting with his superior officers did not take place in any exotic location, but in a small room in the base of Nha Trang (the scene was shot in close-up to further convey the sense of claustrophobia). In this room, a general invites Willard to join him for lunch. The superior officer remarks that if Willard can eat one of the shrimps that are served, he will never have to prove his courage elsewhere. A little black humor that leaves Willard impassive. Willard's interest is not food: he is desperately searching for an expiatory mission that will condemn him.

Willard is well aware that they are in the very middle of a demented war. But before they even reach the mouth of the river, Willard witnesses an attack on a Vietcong village. It is a hallucinatory attack, carried out by a swarm of helicopters equipped with speakers that blast Wagner's "Ride of the Valkyries." Leading this attack is Captain Kilgore (Robert Duvall), who wears a black felt sheriff's hat and who explains that "Wagner scares the hell out of them." These exterminators from the sky are disguised as the new masters of Valhalla. The massacre continues. The entire village will be destroyed by napalm, to the officer's satisfaction. Coppola films the helicopters grazing the surface of the water, like evil insects, whose object of destruction is not the shadows, but peace. In the shot that immediately precedes the attack sequence, Coppola shows a woman, dressed in white, gathering a group of children wearing blue and white uniforms. The peaceful scene has turned to horror.

"If that's how Kilgore fought the war, I began to wonder what they really had against Kurtz," Willard asks himself. "It wasn't just insanity and murder. There was enough of that for everyone."

The boat begins its slow journey up the river and Coppola's presentation of it recalls the trip of the conquistadores on the Amazon in Werner Herzog's *Aguirre*. The voyage becomes a voyage of initiation, "a metaphor," says Coppola, "of the voyage of life that each of us takes within ourselves and during which we choose between good and evil."

But, faced with the spectacle of such destruction, how can you make that choice? Willard sees many other spectacles during his journey. He sees a group of Playboy bunnies dancing in front of thousands of delirious GIs, who are high on alcohol or drugs, or both. He sees soldiers fighting for a worthless bridge in a darkness illuminated only by pointless explosions. All these images accompany Willard during his slow drift along the river.

By reading the confidential material that concerns his mission, Willard slowly uncovers Kurtz's personality. Kurtz was a senior officer with an excellent service record who was on his way to the highest ranks and honors. Then, one day, he snapped. Following an inspection tour in Vietnam, Kurtz filed a restricted and explosive report that embarrassed President Johnson and his chiefs of staff. Kurtz then asked to be sent back to Vietnam. Something had broken inside him. Lulled by the movement of the boat and looking at photographs of Kurtz, Willard begins to feel admiration for this man . . . a man who, in order not to follow the rules any longer, had made his own rules. "Never leave the boat. Absolutely goddamn right," says the voice-over, "unless you were going all the way. Kurtz got off the boat. He split from the whole fucking program."

Inside the secret file, Willard discovers that Kurtz had ordered the execution of certain Vietnamese he believed to be double agents. Such assassinations are not unlike Willard's current mission. He too can remember having felt against his cheek the last breath of his victims. Willard begins to feel an obscure kinship with Kurtz. Both men had gone beyond the limits set by civilization, both had commit-

Top: **The smell of napalm in the morning. Robert Duvall.**

Bottom: **Dennis Hopper.**

65

Sam Bottoms, one of the survivors of the "voyage."

Opposite page, top: **The arrival of Willard (Martin Sheen) at Kurtz's hideaway.**

Opposite page, bottom: **Martin Sheen, waiting . . . in *Apocalypse Now*.**

ted crimes without mercy. But Kurtz went further yet, much further, into a realm of horror that begins to attract Willard. Willard becomes obsessed with the desire to discover the secrets of this man and to know what it is to be free of all restraints.

A Slow Death

The answer, the revelation, lies just beyond the next bend in the river. "He was close. He was real close. I couldn't see him yet, but I could feel him," says the voice in a whisper, "as if the boat were being sucked upriver and the water was flowing back into the jungle. Whatever was going to happen, it wasn't going to be the way they called it in Nha Trang."

Willard is suddenly afraid to find himself face to face with this man he has come to know through papers, letters, and a voice on a tape, a voice that echoes strangely.

"Part of me was afraid of what I would find and what I would do once I got there. I knew the risks, or I imagined I knew. The thing I felt the most, much stronger than fear, was the desire to confront him."

The boat finally reaches its destination. Kurtz's realm, amidst the ruins of Angkor, is reminiscent of Jim Jones's Guyana. Willard and his crew are met by a group of stray soldiers and natives, united in this savage state.

As Willard arrives at Kurtz's lair, Coppola also reaches the crucial point of his mission. The film has shifted slightly, changing to that metaphysical quest so dear to Anglo-Saxon novelists. In the way that the character in Jack London's *Sea Wolf* hunts down his brother across the ocean, Willard has given chase to his own identity, in this trip up the river, in this search for the soldier of fortune who has chosen the jungle as the irrational empire of his dissidence.

"Everything I saw told me that Kurtz had gone insane," says the voice. "The place was full of bodies, North Vietnamese, Vietcong, Cambodians. If I was still alive, it was because he wanted me that way. It smelled like slow death in there, malaria, nightmares. This was the end of the river all right."

Coppola's approach is clear: "I wanted to begin with a dream, then proceed on. I thought audiences were familiar with war films and I wanted to first gain their confidence and then have them accompany me on a journey, for this is not a film, but a journey."

But we have not yet reached the end of the journey. With the help of a photojournalist, a veritable rag of a man who lives in Kurtz's shadow, Willard finally meets the colonel. Even in his delirium, Kurtz has understood the purpose of Willard's mission.

But first, he will talk, and tell his story from the shadow of his refuge. He is like a Buddhist priest, whose polished scalp reflects the only light in his dark abode. In his gripping tale, he reveals the reasons for his behavior. He tells of the consequences of a particularly bloody episode: the enemy has penetrated a camp in which the Americans had inoculated Vietnamese children. To show their displeasure, "they," the enemy, had come into the camp and "hacked off every inoculated arm," and piled them up in a hideous accusatory mound. This devastating episode confirmed to Kurtz the fact that Americans were incapable of finding a solution to the war. They lacked the ability and especially the moral strength to fight such a determined enemy.

Willard had also understood this: it was the message of a man called to his destiny, and Coppola, speaking through Kurtz, offers his own views of America's failure in Vietnam.

Before confronting the man with whom he has increasingly identified, Willard is captured, tortured, and locked in a bamboo cage. The decapitated head of one of his men is thrown into the cage.

"Are you an assassin?" asks Kurtz. "I am a soldier," replies Willard.

"You're neither," answers Kurtz, "you are an errand boy sent by grocery clerks to collect the bill." Kurtz has understood Willard's true nature. He does not fit into the Conradian scheme, he is not faithful to the laws of the ocean. He will kill Kurtz rather than save him precisely because his orders have been countersigned by the victim himself!

The New Master

The atrocities described by Kurtz are never shown, nor do we ever see Kurtz's men in action. This actually increases the impact of Kurtz's story.

In John Milius's original script, Kurtz's commandos would leap from the bushes, like animals, to attack the enemy.

"On the river, I thought that the minute I'd look at him, I'd know what

The only light reflects on Marlon Brando's head.

to do, but it didn't happen. I was in there with him for days, not under guard. I was free, but he knew I wasn't going anywhere. He knew more about what I was going to do than I did."

Because of their respective and common experiences, Kurtz and Willard represent two facets of the same man. And the death of one by the hand of the other is actually a form of deliverance. Yes, deliverance. As Kurtz's strength diminishes, he must, in the way of ancient rituals, be killed by a younger and stronger man, so that his power (upon which rests the world's stability) will not be lost. "Everybody wanted me to do it, him most of all," says Willard's voice. "I felt like he was out there, waiting for me to take the pain away. He just wanted to go out like a soldier, not like some poor, wasted, rag-assed renegade. Even the

jungle wanted him dead, and that's who he really took his orders from anyway." Entrusted by Kurtz with bringing Kurtz's will back to his son, Willard returns to the boat. Outside, Kurtz's people bow to him: he is their new master. An ending that caused Coppola to suffer in the depths of uncertainty for many months.

One of the other endings that had been considered involved a siege on Kurtz's domain, carried out by American and Vietnamese troops. This stylized sequence would have been in step with the film's title. A storyboard had been drawn of it, and Coppola had even started to film part of it before abandoning that version.

"The film ends with a moral choice," explained Coppola, when the film was presented in Cannes. "Will Willard become another Kurtz? Or

will he learn from his experience and choose another direction? I wanted to leave the end open. I filmed the other ending, and that was the one I would have preferred, but I am not sure that it was what Willard would have done. As I cannot lie, I could not use it. There is a sentence in *Heart of Darkness* that says: 'Above all, what I cannot bear is the stench of lies.' "

The definitive version shows Willard returning toward the river while the credits roll, in the 35-millimeter version, with napalm explosions going on in the background. "This film illustrates the exceptional case of a man who has gone beyond the usual human limitations," affirms Coppola. "He goes too far and is destroyed. In one sense, Kurtz's death is a sacrifice, a sacrifice for America. I wanted America to see the face of horror and accept it as its own. Only then can it go forward." Coppola speaks of the future, of a past that must be exorcised in order to plan and prepare for this future with serenity. But it still does not explain why Coppola, like Willard, remains fascinated by Kurtz.

"A Catharsis for My Anguish"

To understand better what appealed to Coppola, we need to turn to his other films. Coppola's characters fall into two main categories: the Godfathers and the Loners.

In the first category we find, besides Kurtz, Lady Holoran, the dowager in *Dementia 13*, General Patton, and Vito and Michael Corleone.

Natalie Ravenna *(The Rain People)*, Harry Caul *(The Conversation)*, Hank and Franny *(One From the Heart)*, and Rusty James *(Rumble Fish)* are Loners, as is Willard. Both categories are closely linked to their families, whether it be that of the Mafia in *The Godfather* or the army in *Apocalypse Now*.

These Godfathers rule over their families (who are often killers themselves) as demigods.

The Loners, on the other hand, try to break these family ties (Harry Caul), to run away from them (Natalie Ravenna), or to replace them with something else (Michael Corleone and Willard). But the distinction between the Godfathers and the Loners is never an absolute one. Michael Corleone is a Loner at the beginning of *The Godfather,* when he tries to avoid any involvement with the "family business," and becomes a Godfather at the end of the film. But in *The Godfather, Part II,* when he has eliminated all of his enemies, he will once again become a Loner.

Similarly, Kurtz goes from one state to the other. In *Apocalypse Now,* Kurtz is a desperate Godfather who is incapable of satisfying his deepest desires. He is waiting for the Loner who will

Marlon Brando and Martin Sheen. The death of the double.

relieve him, only to become, perhaps, another Godfather.

In Orson Welles's aborted version of *Heart of Darkness,* there would undoubtedly have been many parallels drawn between Kurtz and Hitler (the time at which the filming would have occurred would have forced him to take such a historical perspective), but also between Kurtz and Welles. Coppola himself did not escape the spell of Kurtz's jungle.

"The film developed on its own, as we were going along," says Coppola. "And the shooting began to resemble the film itself. I soon realized that the ideas and images I was trying to put on the screen coincided with certain aspects of my own life. Like Willard lost in the jungle, I was traveling along the river, hoping to find answers to my questions and a catharsis for my anguish."

Coppola did not just make films about Godfathers: he became one. For years, he worked at becoming a Prometheus attached on one side to his role as an artist of merit, and on the other to his role as the new owner of a small private empire in the fashion of Louis B. Mayer or Harry Cohn. With the difference that Coppola wanted to use his power to realize ambitious artistic ideals. He is not different from Kurtz, and he too has an extended family, of whom he could be king.

Let us return to one of the film's most powerful scenes, that of the attack on the small coastal village by the helicopters. What one senses above all is the large-scale maneuvers of modern combat. Coppola's masterful agility and ability are superbly demonstrated in this sequence. Kilgore adds a touch of involuntary humor when, after the assault, he breathes the smell of napalm and exults: "It smells . . . like victory." This jubilation is also Coppola's. Until this point, the artistic dimension of the film was as equivocal as the million-dollar combat scenes. Coppola has been leading his armies of technicians on their own battlefields, and once the sequence is masterfully edited and mixed, Coppola's victory is as sweet as Kilgore's.

In his comparison of the sister technologies of war and cinema, Coppola parodies Hitchcock by including himself in a short sequence in the film. There he is, directing a television news crew, screaming at the bewildered soldiers not to look into the camera.

A River Movie

Coppola never claimed to offer any political message on the war. He never attempted to explain the United States' involvement in Vietnam, as many other American films did. There are several sequences in which Americans are seen committing atrocities, but Coppola avoided showing the reality of the war from the Vietnamese point of view.

"I had no intention of making a film whose 'set' was Vietnam. I wanted the audience to leave the theater knowing what Vietnam had been like," explains Coppola. "I wanted them to have experienced it rather than simply to have watched an action film." He adds that he felt he had no right to speak for the Vietnamese: "I could imagine them in a field, planting rice while their children are at school, when suddenly thirty helicopters fly over their heads and drop bombs on them. . . . I could imagine them looking at us, as we were being offered food and women. Other than that, I don't pretend to know what it was like for the Vietnamese, and it would be pretentious of me to include it in the film. That is the subject of another film, to be made by a Vietnamese director."

This explains the impact and strength of *Apocalypse Now,* as compared to other war films such as Hal Ashby's *Coming Home* or Michael Cimino's *The Deer Hunter.* These last two films are classic examples of dramas seeking immediate spectacular effects. *Apocalypse* is far removed from *The Deer Hunter*'s partial and shocking portrayal of Vietnam.

"Apocalypse," adds Coppola, "represents a certain moral dilemma which has always confronted man, and prob-

ably always will. It is the tightrope on which we walk and which links good and evil, right and wrong." One can hear the echo of the first pages of Nietzsche's *Thus Spake Zarathustra.*

Coppola has invented a new grammar of film, and renewed cinematographic writing.

Apocalypse Now is a river movie, in the way that *Easy Rider* was a road movie. It takes us along a river through and toward the immensity of the jungle, showing us the strangeness of its mysterious banks, under a sky of bomb-filled planes that are reflected in the luminescent waters below.

The large budget of *Apocalypse Now* placed Coppola in an awkward situation. Although *Apocalypse Now* was not the only large-budget film of the period, it was quite unlike the others: *Moonraker* ($32,000,000), *Flash Gordon* ($35,000,000), and *Star Trek* ($40,000,000).

Coppola's scale is on the level of artistic fantasy that can only be realized by a certain kind of director. A film with the scope of *Apocalypse Now* is the result of tremendous reflection about greatness, significance, and art. As we have already said, art remains as equivocal a concept as that of the American war in Vietnam. This frustration is reflected in Kurtz's face. Like Coppola, he has gone beyond his own limits in his quest for, not happiness, but a kind of permanent exaltation, which remains unattainable. Many of Coppola's characters are afflicted with the realization that life is fundamentally futile and disappointing.

When Willard, the Loner, kills Kurtz, the Godfather, he is actually freeing Kurtz from his despair and from his unbearable loneliness. Symbolically, it is perhaps Coppola the Godfather who dies at the hand of Coppola the Loner, in memory of the time when he was merely an "artist."

To the very end . . .

Deliverance.

The eye of the master.

8 City Lights

Zoetrope Studios

After the presentation of *Apocalypse Now* at Cannes, Coppola professed the desire to work with an old-fashioned studio, thinking back on the glorious days of MGM. "There are many films in my head, some of which are truly fantastic, but I could only do them with the help of a machine. A studio is a machine and I am going to try to build one. Of course, it is a question of several hundred million dollars, and I cannot do it on my own. I will have to find seven or eight directors with whom to share this adventure."

Building a viable and profitable studio was another way for Coppola to humor his inclination toward patriarchy.

He wanted this studio, and he got it! In 1980 Coppola purchased, for the sum of seven million dollars, the former studios of Hollywood General, in the very heart of Hollywood. The studio consisted of nine stages, thirty-four editing rooms, several bungalows that served as offices and dressing rooms, a special-effects department, wind machines, and curtains, not to mention the curtains and background drops of another time. He renamed the studio Zoetrope Studios.

The Hollywood General Studios had been built in 1919 by John Jasper. At the time, his studios were revolu-tionary and allowed night and day scenes to be shot at will thanks to a specially devised system of sliding shutters.

For the nostalgia buffs, the memory of those who once worked on these stages could still be felt: King Vidor, Harold Lloyd (who directed *Grandma's Boy* there in 1922), Howard Hughes (who filmed a good part of *Hell's Angels* in the studios). During the 1930s, Mae West starred there in *Go West, Young Man,* directed by Henry Hathaway, and Bing Crosby appeared in *Pennies from Heaven.* In later years, James Cagney and his production company took over the studios.

As of 1951, the studio was used exclusively as the set for the "I Love Lucy" show, with Lucille Ball and Desi Arnaz.

Coppola's intention was to "create a real studio, to bring together talented people who could handle every aspect of the film business. The studio was to be their home and would employ them year-round, without interruption." Coppola continues: "I want to give them the studio I never had and always wanted when I was a screenwriter and a director. This feeling of being part of a family, this closeness, would be stimulating to professionals and others alike." Coppola went to work immediately. The studio was rented for the production of *Xanadu,* a musical comedy starring Gene Kelly, and for the production of Richard's Fleicher's *The Jazz Singer,* starring Neil Diamond.

But *Hammett* was the first Zoetrope production that was produced in the studios. Dean Tavoularis built the sets, recreating San Francisco during the 1920s, for Wim Wenders's film about the celebrated mystery writer.

The studio could not function without actors. Sam Bottoms, Larry Fishburne, and Albert Hall had been under contract since *Apocalypse Now.* They were joined by Teri Garr, Frederic Forrest, and Raul Julia, who had signed nonexclusive contracts with Zoetrope.

They in turn were joined by Nastassia Kinski, Harry Dean Stanton, and Lainie Kazan. Dennis Klein, Bill Bowers, and Dennis O'Flaherty signed on as screenwriters. Dean Tavoularis was the set designer and art director and Walter Murch was in charge of the sound department. Tom Luddy, a renowned film historian and authority, was in charge of "special projects." It was Luddy who arranged the worldwide premiere of Kurosawa's *Kagemusha* and the American distribution of Hans-Jürgen Syberberg's *Our Hitler* and Jean-Luc Godard's *Every Man for Himself* as well as the restoration and presentation of Abel Gance's *Napoléon.*

Coppola also intended to create a museum within the studio as well as a school that would offer education programs to young people (ages fourteen

The walls of the dream. (Raymond Depardon/Magnum)

to eighteen). Such a program had already been started in San Francisco under the direction of Francis's older brother August.

Michael Powell, the veteran director of such classics as *The Thief of Bagdad, Black Narcissus,* and *The Red Shoes,* was appointed "artist-in-residence" at Zoetrope Studios. Gene Kelly agreed to head the departments of development and musical production. Rudi Fehr was named director of postproduction, and Max Bercutt, a public relations expert, was in charge of the marketing department. Robert Spottia was the studio's director.

Imperious and Vague Demands

There were numerous projects in the works: Zoetrope was financing **The** **Black Stallion,** which was directed by Caroll Ballard, one of Coppola's former classmates at UCLA, and **The Escape Artist,** directed by Caleb Deschanel. Zoetrope was always looking for new talent: after seeing Fielder Cook's made-for-television movie **Too Far to Go** (based on a collection of stories by Pulitzer-prize-winning novelist John Updike), Tom Luddy called Coppola's attention both to the film and to its director. Coppola, impressed by the film, decided to release it in movie theaters. In the fall of 1981, Cook and Coppola cut a new and longer version of the film: they added some special effects before completing the mix in San Francisco. On April 23, 1982, **Too Far to Go** was released in a theater in New York under the Zoetrope label before being presented at the Quinzaine des Réalisateurs in Cannes during the month of May.

Problems began during the extended shooting of **One From the Heart.** After five months of rehearsals, in February 1981, the foreign investors, who were supposed to invest seven million dollars (the remaining eight million being borrowed from Chase Manhattan), withdrew their money when they became frightened by the estimated cost overruns (the original budget was projected at fifteen million but rapidly increased to twenty-three). The specter of **Apocalypse Now** was still about, and all of Hollywood lived in fear of another catastrophe like Michael Cimino's film **Heaven's Gate,** a film that cost thirty-six million. The film's unmitigated failure had made investors far more cautious than ever before.

On February 4, to restore calm and confidence, Coppola organized a press conference on the very set of **One from the Heart.** He gave a splendid perfor-

74

mance before the two hundred attending journalists. He explained at great length the faith he had in electronics, and never once mentioned his financial difficulties.

The following day, he was unable to meet his weekly payroll of $600,000. In a scene reminiscent of Frank Capra's films, his employees voted to continue their work, without any salary, until the situation could be straightened out. The unions agreed to wait just a few more days.

One of the causes of these financial problems was the bad start of Wim Wenders's *Hammett*. Three successive screenwriters could not write a story that met Coppola's imperious and vague demands. The film's production had begun in the fall of 1980 and was suspended in the spring of 1981. Coppola considered dropping the project altogether, then reshot seventy percent of it in twenty-three hours!

Following the resounding failure of *One from the Heart,* Coppola retreated to the desert, far from Hollywood, and far also from Zoetrope, so as not to hear the nasty snickers made at his expense. Everyone was waiting for David O. Selznick's prophecy to come true: "Hollywood is like Egypt, with all of its crumbling pyramids, whose irreversible degradation will continue until the day when the wind will finally disintegrate the foundations of the last studio into the sand."

One from the Heart

Apocalypse Now played a part in Coppola's decision to direct *One from the Heart:* "One day I was standing in mud up to my neck; there were five helicopters flying above me, and no way of knowing whether they were on camera; seven cameras had been set up and were shooting each other! Each change in scenery began to look like an actual debarcation! I thought to myself that there must be another way to work and I decided that I would never again make a film like this one . . ."

This was Coppola's resolution, made deep in the mud of *Apocalypse Now*. He wanted to go once again into man's "heart of darkness," but with today's state-of-the-art technology, using equipment that had, until then, been used only experimentally. That day, in the mud, he had made a decision, unknowingly, that would take the cinema "one giant step forward."

In early 1980, Coppola went to Japan to present *Apocalypse Now,* and began working on an immense project that, according to him, would take nearly ten years to realize. It consisted of a series of four films inspired by Goethe's *Elective Affinities*. This was to be an enormous endeavor for which all of his previous films had laid a foundation. In brief, the project was the story of a married couple and their involvement with another man and another woman. The four episodes would take place during four very different periods of history, in America and Japan, the West and the East. Coppola explains: "I was walking through the streets of Tokyo reading Goethe and Mishima, and every evening I went to the Kabuki. I was going through a difficult time, I was lonely and I was trying to stay afloat. That's when I received Armyan Bernstein's script, which was set in Chicago. It was the story of two couples, told in a very nice and simple manner. Walking through the Ginza, which is the center of Tokyo and very similar to Las Vegas, I said to myself: What if we moved this story to Las Vegas? For Las Vegas is the ultimate frontier in the United States. It was constructed after all the other cities. It was built on two notions, those of life and luck, which are perhaps the best definition of love."

Coppola decided then and there to film *One from the Heart* not in Chicago but in Las Vegas, and he decided to abandon the psychological aspect and

Fielder Cook, the producer of *Too Far to Go,* with Francis Coppola, in front of Harold Lloyd's bungalow at Zoetrope Studios.

Frederic Forrest and Teri Garr in *One from the Heart*.

film it "in the style of a Kabuki show."

Francis's Mini-Apocalypse

Soon after his return to the States, Coppola was contacted by Governor Jerry Brown. The politician, in preparation for the primary election in Wisconsin, asked Coppola for his help in directing and taping his campaign speech. Coppola had wanted to organize a big rally in front of the Capitol for the occasion, and have it rebroadcast on television. During the Governor's speech, a gigantic Eidiphor system would display a videotape. A sprawling vision of America would illustrate Brown's political message. Coppola had only five days to put this colossal project together. He rented an old video truck, and the whole Zoetrope clan, including Dean Tavoularis,

the "family set designer," left for Madison. When the moment for the speech arrived, Coppola was in his truck, and the helicopter that was filming the crowd began descending. The title read LIVE FROM MADISON, but with a terrible spelling mistake! They had to begin all over again. The equipment that had been rented in haste had not been tested. The first part of the show went well despite all the problems, but the second part did not. The technical team soon lost the picture completely. Coppola screamed and hit the equipment, and the radio stopped functioning. Then the projector broke down: the images that were to be projected behind Jerry Brown were now being projected directly on his face. "It was one of the most hilarious spectacles I have ever seen. It looked as if he were receiving a secret transmission from Mars! It was one of the most amazing evenings of my life," recounts Coppola.

It was not surprising that some referred to this event as "Francis's mini-apocalypse."

A great deal of money was lost in this project, as the video was finally completed just before Governor Brown decided to drop out of the presidential race.

Coppola nevertheless managed to draw one constructive conclusion from this incredible experience. He decided to make a film in which he could use the most sophisticated electronic equipment, which would enable him to control all of the film's components: image, sound, mixing . . . *One from the Heart* would be that film. He wanted to shoot the film in Las Vegas, but, rather than simply have successive outdoor shots, he wanted to "direct a total show, in the way you would film a baseball game."

Because of the similarities between the themes of *One from the Heart* and *Elective Affinities*, Coppola saw this as a good way to prepare for his dream project. In *One from the Heart,* Coppola concentrated on the synthesis of theatrical and musical elements, the perfect introduction for the opera represented by *Elective Affinities.*

A Disney Film for Adults

Coppola explains the film's motivations and what he hoped the film would express: "With *One from the Heart,* I tried to come back to certain things I had abandoned along the way. When I was younger, what I wrote was much more romantic, theatrical, and lyrical. I learned to read before I went to school, and my first books were fairy tales and comic books. I wanted to make a film of that style. *One from the Heart* is a romantic-realistic fable, a Disney film for adults."

The film is set in Las Vegas, during the Fourth of July weekend. Franny (Teri Garr) and Hank (Frederic Forrest), who live together but are not married, are celebrating the fifth anniversary of their first meeting. But the difficulties of the relationship are apparent. Franny complains that Hank has gained weight and does not want to make love often enough. Hank tells Franny that she also has let herself go. The monotony of their existence has eaten away at their love. The fight subsides. Franny wants to go out, but "to go out," not just to go to a restaurant as they usually do. In a moment of reconciliation, they make love, but soon begin fighting again. Franny leaves and goes to stay with her friend Maggie, with whom she works in a travel agency. As for Hank, he goes to see his friend Moe, to clear up a few things (Franny had told him that Moe kissed her during a New Year's Eve celebration). Hank and Moe have it out, and Hank spends the night at his friend's house.

The next day, Franny goes to work as usual in the travel agency. As she often does, she begins to dream of far-off places, such as Bora Bora. While she is redecorating the window, a

A moment of tenderness between Franny and Hank.

handsome stranger stops to talk to her. His name is Ray (Raul Julia) and he tells her that he has been to Bora Bora. Ray invites Franny to come see him at the club where he sings and plays the piano. With mixed emotions, Franny agrees to go see him.

Meanwhile, Hank tells Moe of his doubts and problems in the junkyard which they both own. Torn between his guilt and his aspirations, Hank walks through the neon streets of Las Vegas. In the crowd, Moe notices a young German acrobat who seems interested in Hank. Hank offers her a light. The young woman, whose name is Leila, asks Hank to meet her later that evening. Hank cannot get over his luck. He too thinks he is dreaming.

Franny returns home to pack her things and get dressed to meet Ray. Hank, who is there, is surprised by her decision. She goes to meet Ray at the club but discovers that he is only a waiter there. While Franny and Ray are talking, Ray's boss appears. Ray, irritated by the man's tone, quits. Ray and Franny then go dancing in the deserted nightclub, pretending they are in Bora Bora. Then they walk out into the sizzling streets that are crowded with party-goers.

In the meantime, Hank has taken Leila to his "universe," the strange junkyard. The young acrobat performs—and for the last time, she claims—her special high-wire act for him. Then they fall into each other's arms. . . .

As day breaks, regrets surface. Leila, who is disappointed, will disappear "like spit on a griddle." Hank, who has been looking all over for Franny, finally finds her in Ray's motel room. Enraged, he carries her off, half-naked, over his shoulder. In the car, as they are driving home and fighting, Franny tells Hank that she likes Ray because he does not scream at her. Instead, he sings old-fashioned songs to her, something that Hank would never think or dare to do. She tells him that she is leaving for good, and leaving Las Vegas as well. She has decided to go to Bora Bora with Ray.

Hank, hurt and disoriented, rushes to McCarran Airport in time to catch the lovers as they are boarding the plane. As the crowd pushes around him, Hank begins to sing "You Are My Sunshine" to Franny in a breaking voice that can only come from the heart. Franny, who is touched, goes nevertheless.

Hank, in despair, leaves the airport and gets caught in a sudden downpour. He returns home, throws himself on the bed, then begins to burn some of Franny's belongings. But a car stops outside the house. Franny has come back. The house lights up as if by magic . . .

"To Adapt Las Vegas for My Film"

Originally, the screenplay for *One from the Heart* was not a musical and took place in Chicago. When Coppola agreed to direct the film, it was on the condition that he could change it into a musical and set the story in Las Vegas. "With its polarity of magic, of twinkling lights, of reality, of deception, and of everything that concerns the notion of luck, Las Vegas seemed like the perfect setting for a love story. The town itself is a metaphor for love. . . . I want the film *to be* the emotions of these people, in the same way that *Apocalypse Now* was the war. I wanted the public to experience *Apocalypse Now* as if it were experiencing the war. I am interested in films that *are* what they *speak about* . . ."

Coppola then made an adventurous, risky, costly, but eminently creative choice: he decided not to shoot the film on location in Las Vegas, but to recreate the gambling capital in Zoetrope Studios. Coppola justified this decision that many thought was insane: "*One from the Heart* could only be filmed in a studio. Each set is artificial, each set is built and painted to meet the need of that particular moment in the film. We could have shot the film in Las Vegas, but we would have had to rewrite the screenplay to

An irresistible temptation.

fit the town. I wanted to do the opposite: to adapt Las Vegas to my film. All the sets, all the lighting, all the colors were expressly conceived for this story."

This colossal act of defiance was redeemed by the team's prestigious set designer, Dean Tavoularis, who had received an Oscar for his work in *The Godfather, Part II*. For *One from the Heart,* he conceived probably one of the most fascinating sets in the entire history of the cinema. He recreated every aspect of one of the most famous streets in the world: "the Strip" of casinos on Fremont Street. An enormous task, when one realizes that that particular spot is decorated with 125,000 lights and ten miles of neon!

In addition to the blinking lights of Las Vegas, Tavoularis created and supervised the construction of a residential neighborhood (complete with paved streets), of the junkyard (situated in the heart of the desert of Death

Opposite page, top: **All together: Teri Garr, Harry Dean Stanton, Frederic Forrest, and Lainie Kazan.**

Opposite page, bottom: **Franny and Ray's dream window.**

Valley, which was also recreated), of the motel, of the obviously fictitious decor of Bora Bora, of the mind-boggling replica of McCarran Airport, and of the famous hotel strip.

Greg Jein (who had worked on *Close Encounters of the Third Kind* and *Star Trek*) built small-scale models from Tavoularis's designs. He thus reproduced the smallest-scale version of Las Vegas that had ever been made. The neon lights on Fremont Street measure no more than two millimeters in diameter (which is roughly a third smaller than the usual scale).

This impressionist vision of Las Vegas—this universe that is halfway between magic and psychedelia—necessitated the use of models. Jein confirmed this: "We had to build toys that looked alive."

These models were used especially for the process shots (in which film is projected behind the actors to simulate movement), specifically the two sequences on the highway. A ninety-foot platform was built to support several dozen models of apartment houses, restaurants, schools, factories, and motels, whose lighting was individually controlled. A track permitted the camera to move laterally along this platform, just a few inches above the "pavement," at a speed that could go from ten to sixty miles per hour, as needed.

A cyclorama that represented the sky and the mountains of Las Vegas, positioned in the background, would move at the same speed as the camera, to create the effect of movement. Finally, several of the sequences involving the models were shot with a crane, in order to "snake" through the different elements of the set. In these instances, a special lens was fitted to the camera, one that had variable focusing abilities, and that could be operated by remote control.

The director of photography was Vittorio Storaro, an Italian who had won an Oscar for his admirable work on *Apocalypse Now*. His task was to give theatrical stylization to the project.

Having the entire film shot within the walls of Zoetrope Studios permitted Coppola to exercise control over the environment of the production of the film—something that would have been inconceivable during the filming of *Apocalypse Now*—and to insist on the stylized and dreamlike quality of this film. "I wanted to take a story that resembled a fairy tale and treat it almost as Disney would in his animated films. . . . If we had shot the film in Las Vegas, it would have been just another film about relationships set in a real place with people getting in and out of taxis and talking about their love problems. I wanted to do something that people had never seen before. . . ."

Coppola could only fulfill his legitimate ambition with the help of the revolutionary electronics and the advances made in video technology. The actual electronic work on *One from the Heart* began when the film was in its rough draft. A team from Zoetrope, headed by Thomas Brown—who was in charge of special effects at Lucasfilms—developed important changes in video technology: they were able to create a direct exchange between film and video, thereby permitting a video cassette, which normally runs at a speed of thirty frames per second, to work with a film, which runs at twenty-four frames per second.

The Genesis of Electronic Cinema

One from the Heart marked an unprecedented achievement in the history of the cinema. It represented the first application of a technology that would radically change the way films were made, from preproduction to the final cut.

On April 9, 1979, during the fifty-first annual Academy Awards, Francis Coppola announced: "We are on the threshold of something that will make the industrial revolution seem like an audition in a small-town theater. I foresee a revolution in communica-

tions that will affect the cinema, the arts, music, digital electronics, and satellites, but most especially, human talent. . . . It will make possible things that the pioneers of cinema—those from whom we have inherited everything—would have thought impossible."

This working method, which had never been practiced before, warrants a closer look. Here then are the main phases of the making of *One from the Heart*.

To begin with, the screenplay was entered into a computer, and saved on diskettes. It was entered as it developed, without any particular chronology, and looked like "a mosaic of paragraphs." The screenplay could then be arranged and rearranged at will, and the most recent version was always readily available.

A storyboard was created from the screenplay. Each shot was drawn, taking into account the angles from which it would be filmed as well as the camera's movements, which were simulated. This represented nearly five hundred drawings, which were then reproduced on videotape to form an "animated" storyboard. This visual tool was then studied by each of the production departments, who added their respective input and contribution.

Then, under Coppola's direction, a soundtrack was made of the actors and the music. This was somewhat reminiscent of the early days of radio. The soundtrack was then synchronized to the images of the storyboard. The result was a first version of the film in its full length.

The actors' rehearsals came next. Polaroid shots taken during these rehearsals progressively replaced the storyboard drawings, which were updated daily. The current version could be seen at any time, but the previous versions were always kept so that any change, correction, elimination, or addition could be accomplished easily.

After these rehearsals, Coppola took all of the actors to Las Vegas so that they would immerse themselves

Las Vegas made at Zoetrope.

Harry Dean Stanton as Moe.

Opposite page, top: **Frederic Forrest as Hank.**

Opposite page, bottom: **Nastassia Kinski as Leila, Hank's fantasy.**

in the peculiar atmosphere of that town. For two days, the team videotaped the details of the city. Once back in the studios, the actors began three weeks of technical rehearsals while the set was being completed.

The actual shooting could not begin until the set was completed. In February 1981 everything was ready, including all of the electronic equipment that had been standing by. Videotape recorders, monitors, and audio transmission systems connected the set to a special trailer (the only one of its kind). This trailer, the Image and Sound Control Vehicle, contained a complete video mixing system that was the actual "brain" of the film. Coppola, who was inside the trailer, was in constant contact with the set and able to monitor the film's progress with the benefit of a global viewpoint. This video trailer, which was built specifically to meet the needs of this film (and which would be used for future films), was equipped with a kitchenette, a bed, and a Jacuzzi. Ready to hit the road!

The filming began. The film cameras were backed up by video cameras that were connected to the trailer, the "heart" of the operation. Coppola and his main camerman used the monitors to control the framing. Using a simple "replay," they were able to select and correct right then and there any changes that had to be made. All of these tapes were instantly integrated into the animated storyboard.

Vittorio Storaro, the director of photography, then rehearsed the most complex camera movements using a video minicamera which served as his viewer. Following this, Garrett Brown would execute the shots with the Steadycam, a device used to stabilize a hand-held camera.

The film takes that were developed in the lab were then transferred to videotape. The edge numbers on the film were "synchronized" with a time code on the videotape before Coppola would begin the edit.

Electronic cinema saved a considerable amount of time at the mixing stage. The editor and the sound-mix-

ing engineer received their material from the set at the same time. Both worked in auxiliary control centers that were connected to the "brain," and could send sound and visual information for an immediate premix. This extraordinary procedure permitted Coppola to see daily rushes that included the music tracks and sound effects.

The editors had immediate access to all of the filmed material. The easy duplication process permitted simultaneous work to be done by more than one person. The editors could work on one tape, while the director worked on another. The cassette format and a portable editing machine made working outside the studio a much simpler task. The work was distributed in a much more efficent manner, and the result was a better and more creative final cut. The storyboard served as the editors' rough draft, while Coppola worked on his own ideas, which were presented to the editors before they decided on the final result.

A Revolution in Progress

The techniques of electronic cinema helped to reduce both the cost and time of production at every stage. At a time when financing had become so difficult and risky, Coppola had found a solution—perhaps the only temporary solution—that would assure the survival of tomorrow's filmmakers, the future creators of cinematographic art.

This revolutionary method of production enabled Coppola to hold a public preview of *One from the Heart* in Seattle, Washington, on March 15, 1981, one month before the filming was actually completed. This afforded Coppola the opportunity to make certain changes that seemed pertinent, based on the audience's reaction. The making of such changes on a film still in production marked a first in the history of the cinema.

As a form of artistic technology, electronic cinema was inevitably constrained to constantly innovate and modify. To reduce further the costs of film production and to enlarge the field of inquiry for film directors, Coppola foresaw the creation of "completely electronic films": the screenplay would be entirely composed on a computer, the storyboarding and even the actual filming would be done with video equipment—with a high-resolution image—with a final transfer from tape to film only for distribution to theaters.

Thomas Brown (who supervised the work of the Zoetrope electronics team) summarized the actual state of Coppola's experimental research: "What we created for *One from the Heart* was a very rough beginning. It was, of course, far ahead of current cinematographic production techniques, but compared to our next system, this one was quite primitive."

Color Symbolism

After his remarkable work on the photography of *Apocalypse Now,* Vittorio Storaro undertook an impassioned research project concerning "writing with light" in preparation for *One from the Heart.* His problem with this film was to bring to life everyday people and give substance to their emotions within a setting that was deliberately an artificial one.

To solve this problem, he turned to the language of colors. The two principal characters, Franny and Hank, were defined by contrasting tonalities that represented distinct yet complementary emotions, further emphasized by the omnipresent lights of Las Vegas. This color scheme was drawn up in close collaboration with Coppola and Tavoularis during the construction of the screenplay. This project was clearly influenced by certain writings of Goethe—and Coppola's admiration for the German author was well known.

Storaro accurately described the fundamental color symbolism in *One from the Heart:* "I see this film as an attempt to reconcile two energizing poles, two opposing realities, whose

Tom Waits.

This One's from the Heart

Coppola first took notice of Tom Waits after hearing his *Foreign Affairs* album. That particular album was made up of a series of poetic images, much like a short film. This both intrigued and seduced Coppola, who then evaluated Waits's talent as a singer-writer-composer.

Coppola contacted Waits and asked him if he would try his hand at the vast and complex task of writing the musical score for *One from the Heart*. The methods of composition and recording were the same as those used in the creation of a record album. Coppola used postsynchronization to its fullest extent at the time of the final mix.

The musical numbers serve as a commentary to the film, a sort of off-scene narration, a distant mirror reflecting the plot. Two voices—one masculine (the inimitable raspiness of Tom Waits) and the other feminine (the pure clarity of Crystal Gayle)—alternate by singing separately or together. This neo-chorus follows the wanderings of Hank and Franny and speaks for them. Waits and Gayle express what the couple cannot in a subtle blend of nostalgic melodies, romantic ballads, and syncopated rhythms, all accompanied by the underlying and ever-present blues. The final ballad, "This One's from the Heart," gives the film its meaning and its ending and restores pure melodrama in the sense intended by Chaplin, that is, the perfect synthesis of drama and music.

Coppola saw this process as a new dimension for his work: *"One from the Heart* represents a new direction I intend to follow in the coming years. By its style and its language it differs from everything I've done until now. It is both a technological breakthrough and a totally new way to work. I see myself more and more as a film 'composer.' All my future films will have a musical element—singing, dancing, more fluid images."*

union forms what we call visible light, or life: male and female, positive and negative, nature and technology, night and day, hot and cold, light and shadow. . . . It is well known that colors that entertain a relationship of 'simultaneous contrast' intensify, growing from a conflict in personalities. They could very well coexist, but they fight each other as if each one was afraid of being dominated by the other, until their motivating energies lead them toward an irresistible union.

"In *One from the Heart,* the theater of this conflict was Las Vegas, where civilization reigns over nature as light does over the desert. At dusk, the sun disappears and we relax our vigilance. Las Vegas rises with the moon and evokes the primitive element. . . . As a symbol of conquest, the color red dominates the town and causes ten-sion to rise. Yellow and orange stimulate the cardiovascular systems. At nightfall, nature calms our emotions. Green, the color of conservation, and the blue of the night have a regenerative effect: they permit the nervous system to reduce its activity. . . . The conflict between purple-blue-green, the colors of introversion, and red-orange-yellow, the colors of extroversion, is revived. The film is a representation, through the colors of the spectrum, of emotions and feelings that characterize the different moments of our lives. . . ."

Based on this, Franny is symbolized by the color red, and Hank, by green.

The Zoetrope Repertory Company

After having purchased the former Hollywood General Studios in Los Angeles in March of 1980 to house Zoetrope, Coppola decided to form his own repertory company. Five of the principal actors in *One from the Heart* were members of the company. Three of them had already been featured in other Zoetrope productions: Frederic Forrest had appeared in the title role of Wim Wenders's *Hammett*, Teri Garr in Carroll Ballard's *The Black Stallion*, and Raul Julia in Caleb Deschanel's *The Escape Artist*. Nastassia Kinski joined the group after meeting with Coppola during the presentation of *Tess* in Cannes. Lainie Kazan had been involved in several musical productions organized by Coppola when he was a student at Hofstra University in New York.

Attention should be drawn to the professional performances of all these actors, who patiently rehearsed for five months before any actual filming began. The constraints of such a meticulous preparation and the discovery of experimental cinematographic methods often caused the actors to question their own personal approach to acting. Only solid training in comedy—or in dance, as in the case of Teri Garr—could facilitate this study. Nastassia Kinski remembers: "With Polanski, I had to stick to the text. Here, I often had to improvise, and I had to acquire the necessary flexibility to do so. Francis likes to say that the actor is the one who determines the pace of the scene, not the director. That was something very new for me." Nastassia remains quite modest about the fact that for several months, she trained as an acrobat with Bob Yerkes's Circus of the Stars in the San Fernando Valley, in preparation for her disconcertingly natural performance in the role of Lelia, the German tightrope walker who represents, for one night, the realization of Hank's dreams ...

The master's voice . . .

Coppola, "the eye that sees everything."

As for the director, Coppola gained some important insight from his directing experience on this film: "Contrary to popular belief, electronic cinema does not go against the actors. It permits them, if they wish, to see immediately what they are doing and to correct it. For that reason, the rehearsals for *One from the Heart* were very much like theatrical rehearsals. The actors can play with time, they can interpret a ten- or twenty-minute scene in its entirety, not in fragments lasting just a few seconds. . . . But, you know, actors and technicians are like the audience: they strongly resist any change. They are used to thinking that if their interpretation is mediocre in the wide shot, they can save it by cutting to the close-up. But in *One from the Heart,* there are no close-ups as such, so that this way of working confused everyone. I had thought that actors—especially those with training in the theater—would be thrilled to be able to play the scene in its entirety, without having to be preoccupied by the camera. But in fact they were quite reticent and would have preferred a more fragmented and reassuring method of filming. That is why, following this experience, I treated the actors a little differently in my next two films, *The Outsiders* and *Rumble Fish.*"

Singing in the Rain, Dancing in the Rain

Within Zoetrope Studios, Gene Kelly was in charge of coordinating all musical productions. But an inexplicable fear on Kelly's part of endangering his reputation led him to hire, for *One from the Heart,* an unknown choreographer by the name of Kenny Ortega, who was his protégé. Kelly remained on the set throughout the production to supervise the work without assuming the artistic responsibility for the film. Inevitable differences of opinion resulted from the fact that three people were working on the same task: Kenny Ortega, Gene Kelly, and, naturally, Francis Coppola.

The overheated streets of Las Vegas.

Coppola wanted the actors constantly to occupy center stage; he even wanted them to dance alone in the deserted streets. Gene Kelly, on the other hand, brought in many dancers, hoping to cover up the technical deficiencies of the actors (what deficiencies? one wonders, after admiring the fancy footwork of both Teri Garr and Raul Julia). Finally, a compromise was reached, but this incited Coppola to add cars, other people, and children to make the scene even more realistic. The original structure of the movie was also modified, at Kelly's suggestion. In the "Coppolian" version, Franny meets Ray, who takes her to his room, where he sings her a song. They dance together, almost going through the walls of the room, and run through the empty streets of Las Vegas. At the end of the film, they dance romantically in a Bora Bora setting.

Then, at a certain moment, a maître d' appears walking through the sand and tells them to return to their places. Gene Kelly felt that this sequence should not take place at the end of the film but in the middle. He ordered the change rather than suggested it. The production team, who greatly admired him, went along with his decision.

After the film was completed, Coppola admitted: "I still do not know whether he was right or wrong."

Hard Knocks

The reaction to *One from the Heart* was icy as never before: contempt and insults were hurled at the "wonder boy." The folly of his experiment and his attempt to radically and irreversibly modify the future of filmmaking would not be forgiven. The monolithic

nature of Hollywood seemed more proverbial than ever. A disillusioned Coppola declared: "I must admit that when *One from the Heart* was released, I was very hurt. I thought I had done good work, that I had undertaken formal research, that I was helping the film industry, that I had been courageous in giving people a chance and in taking risks. In return, I was not told that, for example, the result was not good but that my ideas had been legitimate ones and that I had the right to my own studio. No, on the contrary, they wanted to make me feel that what I was doing was worthless."

After the deplorable—and profoundly unjustified—failure of *One from the Heart,* Coppola tried to understand the reasons for this tragic misadventure. He declared wisely: "With the benefit of hindsight, I realize that having unknown actors in a film that was experimental and unusual was too much of a handicap. That has nothing to do with the real talents of Frederic Forrest and Teri Garr. . . . And yet, I uphold the simplicity of this story, which has happened to all of us—two people separate, each one meets someone new but they end up together. That is why I accepted Armyan Bernstein's screenplay, because of the plot and not because I particularly liked the dialogue. I left the delicacies for the screenwriter, for when he saw the changes I was making, he felt ill at ease. Today, I think I should have written the whole thing myself. I think it would have turned out better. But neither the characters nor the story interested me that much. And if people say that they could feel that, they were right."

If the story and the characters of *One from the Heart* did not overly seduce Coppola, the shooting of the film did serve him, unconsciously at first, then consciously, as a form of therapy, due to the involuntary coincidence of a common story and a marital drama he had just lived through (as described in Eleonor Coppola's notes on *Apocalypse Now)*. Francis explains: "Like everyone else, I had had an experience similar to the one in *One from the Heart*. And, as I was making the film, I remembered it quite vividly. Everyone knows that this sort of situation is no laughing matter, and that love can kill. I therefore directed the film the way I did because I could not directly speak of a breakup, having been through it myself. The twelve-hour days or nights spent crying, the suicide attempts, were still fresh in my mind and I did not want to deal with them. I preferred—as in religion—to find an equivalent of this experience in the form of a ritual. It was probably because the true story was so fresh in my mind that I chose this form of alienation."

At the end of 1983, Coppola was in New York shooting his twelfth film, *The Cotton Club.* He was also getting ready to screen *One from the Heart* in Radio City Music Hall in order to work

on it, to cut it differently perhaps, using parts that had been originally omitted. The film director could still not understand his film's flagrant failure, especially within the United States. Coppola undertook this task because of his special feeling for the film. This did not in any way affect the value of his original conception. It is but another proof of the certain humility of the creator as he awaits the ruthless verdict of the audience.

You Are My Sunshine

One from the Heart is a film that defies description. It is disturbing, and difficult to grasp. Coppola wanted to distance himself from the mediocrity of the Hollywood superproductions. With the financial means that would stop any Hollywood big shot in his tracks, the "wonder boy" chose to tell a story, a simple story. The very essence of the cinema . . . but extreme in its technological makeup and in the resulting image. Quite simply, though, a love story, such as the cinema has so often given us.

But Coppola wants us to remain lucid, for his film is about a breakup, about the emotional split of a couple on the night of the Fourth of July. And Las Vegas, the city of all vices, offers the two lovers a fleeting dream, an impossible dream, as "fake" as the set around it. In fact, the artifice is double, in a reinvented Las Vegas. This mirage of life is confirmed by an illusion of neon in the very heart of the Death Valley desert. The Valley of Death . . . At the threshold of the desert wasteland is the car junkyard, a symbol of overconsumption.

Franny has chosen to walk out on this deadly banality. She has chosen to follow literally her dream of "finally going somewhere" (as she naïvely exclaims in the airport). Where? Bora Bora. Nothing less. It is a matter of survival.

Franny can no longer bear the artificiality of the lights and the glitter. The abolition, the negation of nature has

Nastassia Kinski, Coppola, and Frederic Forrest.

become the negation of life itself. Hank, without realizing it, has also become allergic to this prefabricated atmosphere. Lost in the omnipresent neon, he tells Moe: "You know what's wrong in America? It's the light. . . . There are no more secrets, everything is fake. Nothing is real anymore . . ."

How then do feelings survive? They liquefy in the blinding fairylight of this story-book society. One makes love after covering the night-table lamp . . .

Freud wrote: "The opposite of the game is not seriousness but reality." Las Vegas is a hell full of games, a place where despair can escape from reality. One plays to forget real life. It is not by chance that these delirious festivities—just like the film—avoid the night altogether. Sunlight is far too natural and it restores people and things to their original state, devoid of any artifice. When day breaks, it becomes increasingly difficult to fake the rules. One can cheat at roulette, but not at life.

From its conception to its final distribution, *One from the Heart* remains a fairy tale, which, like all tales, has sad passages that are emotionally disturbing and trying. As in our childhood stories, the test, the "rite of passage"—in this case the momentary separation of Hank and Franny—will teach them a lesson, and they will have learned maturity and wisdom.

The phantoms of the night are chased away by a dawn that is full of hope, a dawn that represents a new beginning. The impossible dream has vanished. If the main characters decide to keep on living, they will do so with their eyes open, in spite of the risks. . . .

Because *One from the Heart* is a magical film, Coppola delights in speaking of his own magic, that is, making films. He pays frequent homage to the important films of our childhood, the genetic basis of the cinema, the magic of our century.

For example, the enormous fake ring that Hank has brought to the car lot: when he shows it to Leila—the little acrobat who "knows how to imagine better than anyone else"—the young girl says without a moment of hesitation: "It is the eye that sees everything." And there is Franny in Ray's arms, in answer to Hank's inner question and legitimate concern. This is how Coppola salutes such films as Michael Powell's *The Thief of Bagdad* (with Sabu and Conrad Veidt), a film shot in the former Hollywood General Studios, that is to say, in what are now Zoetrope Studios. This was not by chance . . . But Coppola begins his tributes even earlier in the film. At the very onset of the film, there is a shot of a NO TRESPASSING sign that is reminiscent of the more frightening one in *Citizen Kane.* Further on, *A Place in the Sun* makes reference to George Stevens's work. As for the sun itself, the quest for true light is set from the start, but it is given in the form of a Sherlock Holmes clue, a kind of "Rosebud" revisited.

All the magnificent memories of the 1940s and 1950s cinema come back to life. Ray, at the piano, reminds us of Bogart as he speaks of Michael Curtiz's *Casablanca,* a story about a woman who is torn between two men. Franny regrets that Bogie lets Ingrid Bergman leave: "He should have

stopped her." Is she thinking of Hank? Further one, we can make out the neon sign that spells out *Mogambo* (by John Ford), the counterpart of *Casablanca,* as it deals with a man torn between two women. Where do Coppola's characters begin? Where does their identification stop? This is big-screen fiction within another big-screen fiction. The story of two mirrors that reflect each other ad infinitum . . . The illuminated ship of Fellini's *Amarcord* whose destination is Bora Bora, childhood. . . .

And there is also—and many critics have failed to see it—a surprising humor in many of the scenes in *One from the Heart.* This humor is also the heritage of the great prewar comedies. One of the funnier scenes takes place when Hank "kidnaps" Franny. There are several camera flashes. Ray, trying to maintain his dignity, carries an ice bucket under his arm as his bathrobe slips open. For a few seconds, he is Cary Grant in the best of Capra's films. There are also the clumsy pirouettes of Hank, as he tries to gain access to Ray's room. Or the way he sobs at Maggie's house, while affirming he no longer cares for Franny. But he leaps from the chair as soon as

Maggie tells him where Franny is . . .

All of this is cleverly and masterfully handled, and is not surprising if one is familiar with Coppola's work in its entirety.

This chapter could not end without a discussion of the final scene, one of the strongest emotional scenes in *One from the Heart.* When Hank arrives at the airport, he begins to sing, perhaps for the first time in his life. He sings without any embarrassment amidst all the passengers, for he is singing for Franny, in an attempt to gain her back. He sings "You Are My Sunshine." But Franny is afraid. A desperate Hank leaves the airport as a storm breaks out, flooding his convertible car. The rain does not conceal the fact that he is crying. There is a vague memory of *The Rain People.* When he reaches his house, Hank collapses on the bed and "melts." But he is forgetting the sun that follows the storm.

When Franny returns from her false departure (in every sense of the word), the lights of the house light up miraculously. The light is soft and unlike any we have seen so far. Outside, day breaks. The sun is still invisible. But Hank and Franny wait for it on their balcony. And it is coming. . . .

Smile of a summer night.

Matt Dillon, C. Thomas Howell, and Ralph Macchio, the three "greaser" heros in *The Outsiders*.

9 Rebel Without a Cause

The Outsiders

After the release and whopping failure—in the United States and abroad—of *One from the Heart,* Francis Ford Coppola began working on the screenplay of *The Outsiders.* The script was based on a well-known novel that was popular with the country's teenage population. The author, a young woman by the name of S. E. Hinton, was only seventeen when her book was first published. The story of how the film came about is worth a detour.

In 1980, Coppola received a letter from the Lone Star Junior High School in Fresno, California. The school's librarian explained in the letter that all her students had chosen Coppola to adapt their favorite book, *The Outsiders,* into a film. These young students felt that only Coppola could be "trusted" to do it correctly.

"The letter was signed Mary, Joe, Louis, Sam. . . . I was very touched and gave the book to Fred Roos, one of my producers, who liked it. . . ." Roos remembers: "I adored the book. Francis had not read it yet, but he adored the letter. I was ready to do anything to get this project going. Francis took his time making up his mind."

Coppola's hesitation could easily be understood given his recent experi-

ence with *One from the Heart.* Also, he had decided to retire and concentrate on writing.

A *Gone with the Wind* for Children

To arouse Coppola's interest and to convince him to return to directing, Fred Roos gathered further information. He learned that four million copies of the *The Outsiders* had been sold in the United States alone. The book had also been translated into seven other languages, including Japanese. Roos finally convinced Coppola to read S. E. Hinton's book. "As I was reading the book, I realized that I wanted to make a film about young people and about belonging. Belonging to a peer group with whom one can identify and for whom one feels real love. And even though these boys are poor and to a certain extent insignificant, the story gives them a kind of beauty and nobility."

Coppola gave in to Roos's enthusiasm. "The book was a kind of *Gone with the Wind* for children, an epic class struggle between the "greasers" and the "socs," that is to say, the poor and the rich during the 1960s. All of the greasers were orphans, all outsiders, but together they formed a family. It is a very sentimental story that all

high school students love and which was studied in class. My idea was that I would no longer direct my work toward the parents but toward their children."

Coppola had reaffirmed to anyone who would listen that he was bored and disappointed by adults. Only children maintained his interest and amazed him repeatedly. The experience of *The Outsiders* confirmed this even more: "All the actors were fifteen or sixteen: they were wonderful. . . . Spending time with the young people encouraged me because they are not cynical. . . . I always got along well with children. I prefer them to adults. I would be happy if I could spend my life with them. . . . In any case, it did me good after the destructive experience of Zoetrope Studios and the hostility I encountered there."

Of all his films, Coppola considers *The Outsiders* to be the most like *The Godfather* because of the emphasis on great exploits, with a mix of intensity and emotion that runs throughout. Coppola also shed some light on the film's (and the novel's) leitmotif of Oklahoma sunsets. As brilliant as they are varied, these sunsets seem suspended in mid-air. For Coppola, they serve as the perfect metaphor for his film: "When you watch the sun set, you realize it is already dying. The same applies to youth. When youth reaches its highest level of perfection,

you can already sense the forces that will destroy it. I wanted to capture that moment, to take these street kids and give them a heroic dimension." To capture this evanescent moment of youth on film, Coppola and Fred Roos—the famous casting director—chose eleven young actors of the same age as those in the story.

C. Thomas Howell, who had been featured in Steven Spielberg's *E.T.*, was chosen for the part of Ponyboy Curtis. Matt Dillon, who had just starred in the Disney production of *Tex* (S. E. Hinton's second novel), portrayed Dallas, Ponyboy's friend and role model. Ralph Macchio delivered a moving performance as the martyred Johnny.

Also appearing in the film were Emilio Estevez (Martin Sheen's son), in the role of Two-bit, as well as Tom Waits and S. E. Hinton, who played the part of the nurse.

A Naturalist Film

Coppola chose one of his former UCLA schoolmates, Steve Burum, as director of photography. Burum and Coppola screened several of Roger Corman's films of the 1960s as well as many Japanese films, including those of Mizoguchi. They spoke of the film's style in terms of Japanese formalism. But the reality of the Oklahoma landscape and the strict shooting schedule (six weeks) soon set their own rules. Burum recalls: "Our location was a collage of interwoven elements with a large number of actors in each scene. We decided to plan the staging around the characters. Everything is altered through someone else's eyes, but at the same time it is developed by Ponyboy since it is his story."

It is important to point out that Ponyboy's viewpoint, as the film's narrator, is a matter of memory, not something that the camera shows. Coppola's ultimate goal was to show that the things one remembers still have a tremendous impact on the present.

As Coppola wished to lend a heroic dimension to the "outsiders," he decided to shoot in wide-screen, using an anamorphic lens. Hence the resulting distortion of certain characters and actions, symbolically similar to that of memory. Steve Burum liked to play with the borders of the screen and the edges of the film: "You have to go beyond the idea of the frame as the proscenium and feel free to tilt the camera if the scene calls for it." *The Outsiders* was shot in its entirety between April and June of 1982 in and around Tulsa, Oklahoma, in the very same area described in the novel. Certain modifications were necessary, though, and Dean Tavoularis created original sets that evoked 1966. He specifically chose deserted and abandoned areas of the city to convey the outcast quality of the greasers.

The rehearsals were filmed in video, in the gymnasium of a college, using a blue background. This permitted the later insertion of the photographs taken of Tulsa. Coppola was thus able to "previsualize" the film as they went along. Coppola himself declared that this film was shot in a very classical, almost traditional manner, in spite of the use of electronic equipment. This time, there was no experimentation . . . Coppola opted again for a purer form of cinema that was closer to a certain reality of daily life.

As he had claimed earlier, Coppola said: "I directed *The Rain People, The Godfather*s, and *The Conversation*. And I think I know what the naturalist style is and how to direct actors in such a way that the audience can identify with the characters." *The Outsiders* fits into the naturalist lineage.

From the very start, Coppola set certain rules as to how the characters of the greasers should be filmed: they had to be presented heroically, with dignity, and with as much humanity as the socs. These instructions were repeated daily not only to the actors but also to the entire technical team. More than anything, Coppola wanted to endow his disadvantaged kids with the greatest human dimension.

The result was a series of stylized images, sometimes of epic proportion, sometimes downright romantic or even bizarre. The characters were always in the foreground, never seen in the distance of visual narrative. Carmine Coppola wrote the film's musical score and declared: "Human emotions are really identical for all individuals, whether they be young or old." He composed special themes for each group of characters, the Curtis brothers, their greaser friends, the "socs," and even a theme for Cherry, the "soc" girl with whom Dallas tries to flirt. The haunting ballad of the opening scene is sung by Stevie Wonder.

"Stay Gold, Ponyboy, Stay Gold!"

The story of *The Outsiders* takes place in Tulsa, Oklahoma, in 1966. Ponyboy, a fourteen-year-old boy, is writing in a composition book: "When I stepped out into the bright sunlight from the darkness of the movie house . . ." He begins to tell the dramatic story in which he is both a participant and a witness, that of the greasers and the socs, two rival groups, the poor and the rich of this oil town.

Ponyboy is a greaser, the youngest of three recently orphaned boys. Darrel, the eldest, works hard to provide for his brothers' needs but reprimands Ponyboy often and harshly for hanging around with his friend Johnny. The middle boy, Sodapop, works in a gas station and tries to make peace between his two brothers. One day, Ponyboy is surrounded by a group of "socs" and is lucky to escape unharmed. But the incident only deepens the hostilities already existing between the two groups. Ponyboy, Johnny, and Dallas, a friend of theirs who has just been released from prison, go to a drive-in the following evening. There, they meet two "soc" girls who have just been fighting with their boyfriends. Dallas begins to flirt roughly with one of the girls, Cherry,

Diane Lane, the pretty "soc."

Opposite page, top: The complete group of "greasers": Emilio Estevez, Rob Lowe, C. Thomas Howell, Matt Dillon, Ralph Macchio, Patrick Swayze, Tom Cruise.

Opposite page, bottom: Ponyboy and Johnny ask Dallas to help them.

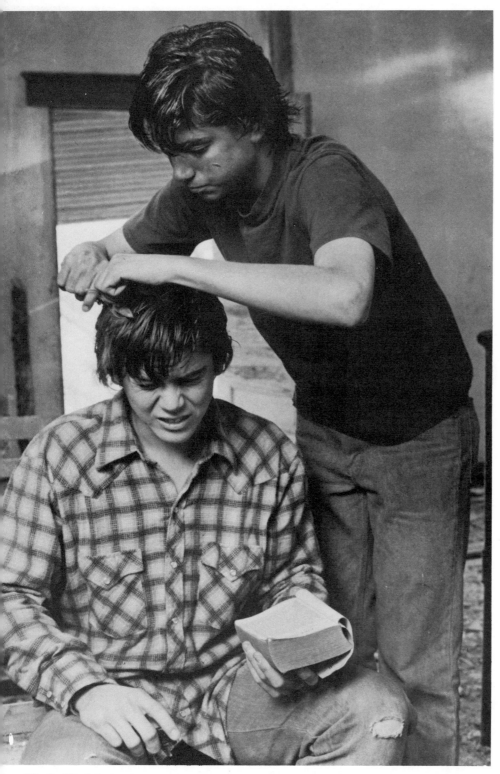

The fugitive's haircut.

who throws her soda in his face. Discouraged, Dallas walks away.

The soc boys see that Ponyboy and Johnny have stayed out late with "their girls." The socs follow them in their Mustang, and an incident is averted only because of Cherry's intervention. When Ponyboy returns home late, Darrel is waiting for him. Ponyboy runs out of the house and joins Johnny, who is sleeping in a field because he is afraid to return to his house. There, they are once again approached by the now drunk socs, who hold Ponyboy's head under the water. Johnny, who has been roughed up, comes forward to help his friend and reaches for his knife.

Later, Ponyboy and Johnny remain alone with the dead body of Bob, the leader of the socs. Johnny sobs: "I killed him." The two friends go to look for Dallas, who gives them money and tells them to go hide in an abandoned church. Armed with enough provisions for eight days, the two boys hide and wait for Dallas. Johnny cuts Ponyboy's hair as well as his own, and, as a further precaution, bleaches Ponyboy's hair. They spend hours reading *Gone with the Wind* and admiring sunsets. Ponyboy recites a poem by Robert Frost that compares childhood innocence to gold . . .

A few days later, Dallas joins them and announces that Cherry has decided to testify on their behalf. He also gives Ponyboy a letter from his brother Sodapop, who tells him that both he and Darrel are concerned about him. The boys decide to surrender to the police. After stopping at a Dairy Queen, the boys notice a fire that has broken out in the church. A group of children who had been picnicking inside are trapped. Listening only to the voice of courage, Johnny and Ponyboy rush to help the children. At the last moment, the roof caves in on Johnny. Ponyboy passes out and Dallas saves them both.

Sodapop and Darrel rush to the hospital to see their brother Ponyboy, who is out of danger. They fall into each other's arms. But Dallas, and

Johnny and Ponyboy play cards while they are hiding out.

especially Johnny, are more seriously hurt. Ponyboy, who has returned home, learns that there is to be a rumble, without weapons, the following evening between the greasers and the socs. Ponyboy and Two-bit tell Dallas about it. While at the hospital, they learn that Johnny's condition is critical. Dallas decides to leave the hospital to take part in the rumble and to take revenge for Johnny. In the pouring rain, the greasers carry an all-out victory over the socs. But the victory is a bitter one, for the next day, Johnny dies in front of Ponyboy and Dallas. Dallas, overwhelmed, and in a moment of madness, holds up a candy store. The police arrive and shoot him down, even though his gun was empty. His friends rush to help him, but it is too late.

Back home, Ponyboy reflects on the entire episode. He leafs through his copy of *Gone with the Wind* and comes across the last letter Johnny had written him before his death. He remembers what Johnny had said in response to Robert Frost's poem: "Stay gold, Ponyboy, stay gold." He also thinks of Dallas, then begins the composition his teacher has asked him to write, based on a personal experience: "When I stepped out into the bright sunlight from the darkness of the movie theater . . ."

"I Would Go See *The Outsiders* Again"

In June 1982, after the filming of *The Outsiders* was completed, Coppola was still unsatisfied with certain scenes which, he felt, were lacking in strength. He ordered some of the sets to be rebuilt, and reshot several sequences. The film's release, which had been scheduled for the fall of 1982, was indefinitely postponed. In the meantime, the Zoetrope Studios were having a difficult time. The debts were accumulating, and the rumors concerning a public auction were circulating more than ever. This situation lasted for five months.

In a similar vein, Warner Bros., who had purchased the rights to *The Outsiders,* announced the film's release, then a postponement. The final release date was set for March 25, 1983, in 829 theaters across the United States. For the first time, a film by Francis Coppola received no formal advance publicity. But information concerning the film had been released to a select public—specifically, the young people. Warner Bros. and Zoetrope concentrated on the specialized magazines and television programs devoted to teenagers. Warner Bros. wanted to market *The Outsiders* as a film for the younger generation. During a preview of the film in Tulsa, nearly half the audience was made up of the city's high school students.

The American critics predicted another failure. Most of them mocked Coppola for having chosen such a simple, if not trite, story. They were therefore shocked when, at the end of the first week, the film's receipts showed earnings of six million dollars, followed by five million the next week. The final earnings were ten times the amount originally invested. The audience continued to flock to the theaters despite the poor reviews. Coppola was continually scorned and insulted by the critics, but this did not affect the film's popularity. The explanation for such a phenomenon can perhaps be best explained by a letter sent to the *Los Angeles Times*. A young boy wrote: "There should be more films like *The Outsiders*. Filmmakers think that young people are only interested in films like *Fast Times at Ridgemont High* or violent films like *Bad Boys*. They think that young people will not go see anything else. We like those films while we are watching them, but we would not go see most of them a second time. *Porky's* was great because it was funny and had a lot of sex, but I cannot even remember the characters. I would not go see *Porky's* a second time, but I would go see *The Outsiders* again."

Oklahoma Sunsets

The American critics considered *The Outsiders* to be a minor film for teenagers suffering from proverbial discontent. They seized this opportunity, once again, to attack Coppola. Vincent Canby of *The New York Times* compared *The Outsiders* to "a remake of *Rebel Without a Cause* by a director who thinks he is D. W. Griffith filming *The Birth of a Nation*."

This remark is not entirely unfounded. Coppola is perhaps the only film director who can create an original work while still paying tribute to past masters, and never stray into areas of plagiarism.

This is because Coppola's films represent a moment in history and because they reflect images of our collec-

Top: **The fire in the abandoned church.**

Bottom: **The three brothers meet at the hospital. Patrick Swayze, C. Thomas Howell, and Rob Lowe.**

Opposite page: **The final battle: Dallas carries Ponyboy.**

tive past. Therefore, Coppola can well be considered to be a new Griffith, working within the framework of the 1980s. The long night that has ended with a flick of the knife is naturally reminiscent of Nicholas Ray's **Rebel Without a Cause**. But there is no plagiarism or imitation here . . .

The escape into the countryside evokes the bucolic foray in Charles Laughton's **Night of the Hunter**. Here, it concerns the wondrous discovery of nature, the dream of a perfect harmony. Golden sunsets abound. Yet the threat to the gold of innocent childhood is close by, as in Robert Frost's poem . . . Evil lurks, and the children know it. In **The Outsiders**, the children are not being hounded by the eager (and brilliant) Robert Mitchum, but by the police, the law of adults which will be the only corrupting force of the film. The results, though, will be identical. "Stay gold, Ponyboy, stay gold." Little Johnny, the victim of an absurd violence, repeated these words until the very end.

This internal class war, this civil war between the greasers and the socs, is but a transposition of another bloody civil war. Exactly the same as in **The Birth of a Nation**, or as in **Gone with the Wind**, which the two boys read avidly while they are in hiding. Once again, there is a feeling of homage or reminiscence in the heart of the film's action. The church fire evokes, within due proportion, the burning of Atlanta.

Those magical sunsets had already reminded us of Victor Fleming's films. But whereas the old Hollywood directors would use traveling shots bursting with music, Coppola uses a much lighter and more delicate approach; still or almost still shots, with a musical score that is more insinuated than actually heard.

These sunsets that constitute the film's leitmotif are the direct opposite of the bright lights in **One from the Heart**. Coppola had already mentioned this: **"One from the Heart** was a film about neon lights; my next film will be about sunsets."** And he knows what he is speaking of in the matter of

lighting. The image actually reverberates! Even the opening titles are golden: a series of photographs taken of Tulsa were reworked with a synthesizer to add golden and incendiary hues.

There are endless reminders of other films in *The Outsiders*. The courage and sacrifice of the two boys who rush to rescue the children trapped in the fire evoke the behavior of John Ford's heroes: people whom no one respects at first and who are more worthy of respect than those who judge them.

Mention should also be made of the influence of the Japanese cinema felt in this film. Coppola especially admired Kurosawa's work, and a certain "sadism" in several of the violent scenes is not coincidental . . .

But mainly, one can find Coppolian references: this obsessive concern with one person's responsibility toward the other, the fragility of people beneath their exterior coarseness. Dallas is seen crying, as disoriented as a child, after Johnny's death. The rumble scene that takes place in the rain is reminiscent of *The Rain People*: "The rain people are made of rain, and when they cry they disappear altogether because they quite dissolve." Ponyboy cries as does Dallas. They are overwhelmed by the death of their friend. By death itself. By Johnny's wish to kill himself at the very beginning of the film.

But in his final agony, and in the testament-letter that he gives to Ponyboy, Johnny has come to understand that life is worth living. Beyond despair, beyond the fear of growing up and no longer being "gold," there is life. He has come to realize what Chaplin upheld in *Limelight*: "If there is anything as inevitable as death, it is life."

Susie Hinton as the nurse, and Matt Dillon.

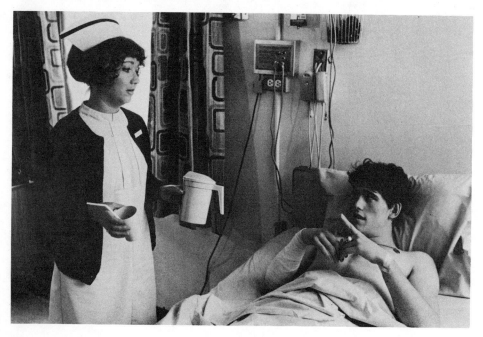

For Dallas, a meeting with death . . .

Rusty James (Matt Dillon) is fascinated by his older brother, the Motorcycle Boy (Mickey Rourke), in *Rumble Fish*.

10 The Heart Is a Lonely Hunter

Rumble Fish

"**W**hile I was filming *The Outsiders*, I decided to make another movie, in a very different spirit—*Rumble Fish*—and I decided to make it in the same place, with the same group of people. I wanted to show that with or without means, with or without stars, with or without new techniques, whatever I did was still Coppola."

Coppola made this decision while he was filming *The Outsiders* during the spring of 1982. His decision caused surprise among his entourage, yet his logic was disarmingly simple.

S. E. Hinton, the author of *The Outsiders*, was a technical adviser on the set. One day, when Coppola was asking her about her other books, she told him about *Rumble Fish*, a book that no one seemed to understand. The book, her third, was selling well, but not as well as the others, *The Outsiders; That Was Then, This Is Now* (written in 1971), the rights to which were purchased by Martin Sheen for his son, Emilio Estevez; and *Tex* (1979), which had been adapted by Disney Films in 1981.

No one seemed to understand what the author was trying to convey in *Rumble Fish*. Except for Matt Dillon, who happened to be starring in *The Outsiders*.

S. E. Hinton had met Matt Dillon in New York even before he appeared in *Tex*. The young actor surprised her when he told her that *Rumble Fish* was his favorite book. Dillon kept saying: "We've got to find someone to buy the book so that I can play Rusty James." Susie (as S. E. Hinton came to be known on the set) told him that it would probably take a long time, and that he might be too old for the part by then. She also asked him if he would then consider playing the role of the Motorcycle Boy. "Yes," he answered, "and if I'm really old, like twenty-seven, I'll direct it." The young man's enthusiasm for the book delighted Susie but shed no further light as to why the public had never shared his feelings.

An Anarchistic Film about Youth

The inspiration for *Rumble Fish* was a disturbing photograph of a young man on a motorcycle that S. E. Hinton had come across in a magazine. This was in 1967, the year *The Outsiders* was published. She cut out the photograph and wrote a short story about it.

Several years later, after the publication of *That Was Then, This Is Now*, she took out the mysterious photograph once again and began to write a novel. "It was as if I had been haunted by a handsome ghost," she said. "The Motorcycle Boy deserved a whole book."

The title *Rumble Fish* intrigued Coppola and reminded him of J. D. Salinger's story "A Good Day for Banana Fish," "a world unto itself."

When Coppola finally got hold of a copy of the book, he realized that it was a very short novel. "I like short novels. I started to read it. Susie had written it when she was much younger—and drunk, I think. . . . This book contained a vision, dialogue, characters that were terrible and truly impressive, as well as very complex ideas. The kind of ideas you don't really understand completely but that you think you understand anyway. The fact that you kept thinking about them is what made it so attractive."

Thrilled by the book, Coppola told the author what he thought. S. E. Hinton recalls: "He told me it was a story for adults, not for children, and he was right. . . . He was the first grown-up I had met who had understood the book."

Coppola saw in *Rumble Fish* the opportunity for an adventurous filming experience. "I wanted to make an anarchistic film about youth, and *Rumble Fish* seemed like the perfect vehicle for the narration of an unusual story."

Coppola and Susie began collaborating on the screenplay of *Rumble Fish* while they were still shooting *The*

Outsiders. They worked hard and often late into the night. There was no improvisation; the "wonder boy's" impassioned perfectionism would never disappear.

When Coppola spoke of this upcoming production, no one took him seriously; *The Outsiders* was still in production, and Zoetrope was now in critical financial shape (in spite of the sale of the studio in April). Everyone told him: "Yes, there is *Rumble Fish*, but let's worry about *The Outsiders*," and they pretended to ignore his project.

When the filming was completed, Coppola took a stronger stand: "I am really going to do it!" But Warner Bros. turned down the project because, according to some, it was afraid the film might compete with *The Outsiders*.

Something Like "Peter and the Wolf"

In July 1982, less than one month after the completion of *The Outsiders*, Coppola began working on his eleventh film. "I think that with *Rumble Fish* we were beginning to have real means of production. We had a very good team, we were full of energy and enthusiasm . . . And everyone was ready to remake cinema!"

As a means of catharsis and because of his creative anguish, Coppola kept cracking jokes about *Rumble Fish*. He would call it "an existential art film for children," or a work by Camus intended for children. He believed that young people thought of *The Outsiders* as an extravagant epic, full of emotions. But with *Rumble Fish*, he wanted to create something like "Peter and the Wolf," a film about which people would say: "You see, you can make black-and-white films and with 14-millimeter focal length." And both the music and the soundtrack can be an integral part of the film. The action can be quite convincing although it is

stylized. . . . And wait until the young people see it!"

"It" remains the most complex, surrealistic, and symbolic film Coppola has made. Indescribable, impossible to explain . . . Coppola had said: "*Rumble Fish* will be to *The Outsiders* what *Apocalypse Now* was to *The Godfather*." It was in fact everything that *The Outsiders* was not: an experimental, convulsive, apocalyptic, and stylistically adventurous film.

Why then did he decide to shoot it in Tulsa? Fred Roos, the producer and Coppola's longtime friend, explains: "It was not specifically a 'Tulsa film.' But we were there, and we had all the means of production at our fingertips. Everything was in place and ready. Also, we knew what the weather would be like. Francis wanted that for his film: the dampness, the stifling humidity. It is a tortured, moody film, full of moisture, steam, and smoke. It had to be shot in a steam-bath and that was the result. From the beginning, we renamed the company 'Hot Weather Film Productions.' "

Although the film was shot in Tulsa, the action is not fixed in any specific time frame. The film opens with a shot of rapidly moving clouds in a tormented sky. Then, a sign on which someone has written THE MOTORCYCLE BOY REIGNS. Rusty James (Matt Dillon) is a tough kid, but he is also a dreamer. He has a girlfriend, Patty (Diane Lane), who comes from a more stable background. Rusty James idolizes his older brother, the Motorcycle Boy, and identifies with him; but his brother left town some time ago.

When they are confronted by a rival gang, Rusty James and his friends win the fight. At that very moment, the Motorcycle Boy (Mickey Rourke) appears. No one had expected him to return. In surprise, Rusty James looks away and is cut by a knife. His brother heads for Biff, the rival leader, with his motorcycle. The Motorcycle Boy then returns home with his brother. He tells Rusty James that he has been to California and that he found their mother who had abandoned them long ago.

She is now living with a television producer. Their father (Dennis Hopper), an alcoholic lawyer, asks him: "How was California?" "One laugh after another," replies the Motorcycle Boy.

The town's policeman is not at all pleased by the return of this prodigal brother and speaks to him in a threatening manner. The Motorcycle Boy pays no attention to him. He is practically deaf from the many fights he had when he was younger, in the days when he was a great gang leader . . . He is also color-blind. The only colors he can distinguish are those of the "rumble fish" that he sees in a neighborhood pet store. He sees the colors he imagines. These small fish are, in fact, brilliantly colorful, but they are also voracious, especially toward each other. They fight in duels that result in death. Their fighting instinct is so strong that if they catch sight of their reflection in a mirror, they will attack it to the point of injuring themselves. The Motorcycle Boy feels a kinship with these fish, the only elements of his universe that he sees in color.

The Motorcycle Boy goes through life in a state of profound confusion, with a permanent half-smile on his face, a smile that is very close to tears. His perception of the world is "like a black-and-white TV with the sound turned low." He seems to have reached the most disillusioned state possible. His voice is removed, remote, almost inaudible. Rusty James, who has always wanted to emulate his older brother, is incapable of reading the message that is coming from him. He does not see that his older brother is completely alienated from the rest of the world, that he is totally unable to conform to the norms that surround him. In his own way, the Motorcycle Boy is trying to warn his younger brother.

Rusty James and his friend Steve (Vincent Spano) are ambushed. For a few moments, Rusty James actually believes he is dying. He can feel himself drifting through the air and he can see his friends crying. The Motorcycle

Rusty James and his gang on their way to a fight.

Love duet (Matt Dillon and Diane Lane).

The choreographed fight sequence.

Boy arrives just in time to save the two boys. Later on, he takes Rusty James back to the pet shop where he had seen the rumble fish.

Besides the Motorcycle Boy, the people who make up Rusty James's life are his friend Steve, a "good boy," and Patty, who loves him but is soon disappointed in his behavior.

After finding out about Rusty James's misdoings at a wild party, Patty leaves him and begins dating Smokey, one of Rusty James's friends. Rusty James feels doubly betrayed. After that, he never leaves the Motorcycle Boy, who tells Rusty James he wishes he could have been a better older brother to him.

The Motorcycle Boy is respected by his peer group and loved by Cassandra. He is compared to a "prince" or "royalty in exile." One night, he takes Rusty James back to the pet shop. He breaks down the door and opens all of the cages and sets the animals free. Then he takes hold of the acquarium containing the rumble fish. He wants, as he pointedly explains, to put them back into the nearby river.

The police arrive. One of the policemen, who hates the Motorcycle Boy, shoots and mortally wounds him. The Motorcycle Boy collapses, dying, on the grass. Rusty James breaks down, then grabs hold of the fish and heads toward the river, thus fulfilling his brother's last wish. As the onlookers gather to gawk at the body, Rusty James gets on his brother's motorcycle and rides off. The graffito THE MOTORCYCLE BOY REIGNS is still visible. The film closes on a shot of Rusty James, standing on a beach, surrounded by seagulls, probably somewhere in the West. There, he will come to understand that in order to find his own identify, he will have to face life. Alone.

Disorder and Chaos

Rumble Fish was filmed in black and white with a few clever color special effects. Coppola devised this as a result of the Motorcycle Boy's color-

106

blindness. "It was suggested in the novel, I did not impose it. . . . If we wanted to convey that someone was color-blind, we could use color for a few instants, and then take it away. Then we thought it would be fantastic if only the fish—which serve as a metaphor for the story—were in color."

The black-and-white dimension permitted Coppola to draw a clear difference between this film and the preceding one: "Because when you use the same team in the same location, it is important to point out that it will not be 'business as usual.' "

To make up his team, Coppola assembled a group of "iconoclasts," as he himself called them. Each one was a specialist in his or her field. Thus began a thrilling experimental process. The group, which was made up of a clever mix of people, included: Stewart Copeland (percussionist of the rock group The Police), Michael Smuin (the choreographer), Steve Burum (the director of photography), and Dean Tavoularis (the production designer). Burum and Tavoularis had worked on *The Outsiders* and were already involved in the planning of *Rumble Fish*.

Steve Burum explains: "Because films are a tremendously popular medium, they have been tied up in realism. What is needed is a more abstract expression of emotion. *Rumble Fish* represents a first attempt at breaking through this realism by making more abstract use of emotionally charged images."

Toward the end of the filming of *The Outsiders*, Tavoularis, Burum, and Coppola would meet, often with other members of their team, and study certain films, particularly those of the German expressionists, such as Robert Wiene's *The Cabinet of Dr. Caligari* and F. W. Murnau's *Sunrise*. They were also influenced by Anatole Litvak's film *Decision before Dawn*, which was filmed in Europe at the end of World War II: "The chaotic mental state of the world was reflected in the film, and that is what we wanted for *Rumble Fish*," says Burum.

Coppola created a complete Dada

Top: **The coup de grace for Biff, the leader of the enemy gang.**

Bottom: **The Motorcycle Boy reigns.**

107

Top: The Motorcycle Boy and Rusty James. The elder teaches the younger.

Middle: The Motorcycle Boy talks about California.

Bottom: Matt Dillon faces his father (Dennis Hopper).

universe, with bursts of smoke emanating from invisible sources, with clouds whose swift travel was reflected in the pane of a window, with a clock without hands, with stuffed animals sitting next to real ones. "We wanted to abstract and elevate reality, to freeze these moments in time," explains Dennis Gassner, the graphic designer.

And yet, in spite of this feeling of doom, *Rumble Fish* does convey a ray of hope: there are ways to escape from this apparently hopeless universe, there is a road toward liberty and liberation. To light the path, Tavoularis sets several of the scenes near a river, near main roads, next to railroad tracks or dark tunnels, all of which represent the way out . . .

As Coppola has said—in a tone of jest—the film does represent an existential dilemma: Do we have a choice? And, if we do, what is it? Should we stay or should we go? How much time do we have? And, what exactly is time?

From the very beginning of this endeavor, Coppola was preoccupied by the notion of time, a preoccupation that has been brilliantly captured in the use of clocks throughout the film.

Coppola recounted a strange anecdote: Susie Hinton, the author of *Rumble Fish,* had seen **The Rain People** years before on television, and was struck by the scene in which James Caan opened all of the animals' cages. She then described an almost identical scene in her book, not realizing that, as a result, Coppola would end up filming the scene again. . . .

A Feeling of Urgency

Coppola was also intrigued by research concerning music and sound. "My fascination for this project resulted in great part from the possibility of weaving a dramatic musical score from the very beginning of the screenplay. Music represents time, the time that is passing by for Rusty James. He must wake up and face reality, or he

will be lost. Style, structure, and music are inextricably linked together."

For some time, Coppola had been contemplating films that would be very different in style from those he was making and even from other directors' films in production. He also had a desire to write his own music. From the very start of the *Rumble Fish* project, Coppola began creating—with the help of his children, his nephews, and their friends—a model for a musical score in a recording studio. He wanted to convey the rapid passage of time, a fact young people never comprehend. To express this concept, Coppola created a rhythm made up of different tempos using all available percussion instruments as well as a bass solo which he performed himself.

He turned to Stewart Copeland "because he is such a marvelous drummer." Coppola said: "His work with The Police showed such precision." Copeland, who had been interested in the cinema for many years, jumped at the chance to be involved in a film production. When he arrived in Tulsa—directly from England—he immediately understood what Coppola was looking for: "Francis wanted to express a feeling of urgency, of time going by. And because time and rhythm are linked, he felt that would help to develop his concept."

Copeland began to improvise. He used an electronic metronome and while the actors were rehearsing, he began looking for the right tempo. "It made me a little crazy sometimes," he remembers.

Copeland proved to be not only a marvelous drummer, but also a natural composer. "Things began to evolve as in a theatrical happening. I was becoming more and more convinced that what he was creating was fantastic," recalls Coppola. "So I backed off and let him proceed alone."

Copeland then recorded street sounds in Tulsa—noises of machinery, traffic, horns, sirens—and added them to the soundtrack. The music was therefore created from authentic sounds, using a new computerized de-

The clock without hands.

vice called Musync, which records the film frame by frame on tape. The film frame itself is recorded on the uppermost band of the tape, the dialogue track is in the middle, and at the very bottom of the tape is space to record the music track.

This fruitful and enthusiastic collaboration pleased Coppola immensely: "Copeland is astonishing!" To which the musician answers: "Coppola is a genius when it comes to generating creativity. He gives you a tremendous margin of working space."

The result of this collaboration was exceptional. The musical score of **Rumble Fish** is one of the most inventive and evocative ever heard in the history of the cinema.

A Beautiful Violence

Another team artist was Michael Smuin, the choreographer and co-director of the San Francisco Ballet. He had directed the successful Broadway production of *Sophisticated Ladies*. Smuin was in charge of "choreographing" the absolutely surrealistic fight between Rusty James and Biff and their respective gangs, as well as the brief dance sequence between the Motorcycle Boy and Cassandra. Coppola chose Smuin becasue he admired Smuin's work in the fight scenes in *Romeo and Juliet* and *Medea*. "He told me that my violence was beautiful," remembers Smuin.

Coppola was determined to have a savage and frenetic fight scene. Tavoularis selected a perfect location, a dark and dingy area, littered with gar-

bage. From there, Smuin could orchestrate the scene as he wished: first, Biff and his gang made a spectacular entrance, appearing on an elevated train platform, emerging from a cloud of smoke. Rusty James swings from a water pipe to avoid being slashed by Biff's knife. The water pipe bursts: sparks fly and frightened pigeons scatter to the sound of a whistling train. Finally, the coup de grace, as conceived by Smuin: after wounding Rusty James, Biff is run down by a "wild" motorcycle. The Motorcycle Boy hurls his empty bike directly at Biff. Coppola loved that sequence!

To achieve the timing of that complex sequence, Matt Dillon and Glen Withrow (Biff) trained with a stuntman.

As for the dance sequence between the Motorcycle Boy and Cassandra,

Top: **Dennis Hopper, the alcoholic but loving father.**

Bottom: **Cassandra (Diana Scarwid).**

Smuin saw it as the young woman's last attempt to renew the relationship she once had with the Motorcycle Boy she still loves. For a few magical moments, it seems to work, but then he walks away. His destiny cannot be linked to anyone else's.

To maintain the emotional intensity throughout the film, Coppola and Burum used intricate camera shots and overlapping scenes. Often, when one character is speaking, the audience strives to see the other person's reaction, a "live theater" tactic, so dear to Coppola.

Love at First Sight

The casting of *Rumble Fish* was obvious: Matt Dillon, because of his long-time interest in the book, was the logical choice for Rusty James. Having just completed *The Outsiders,* he was also in the right "frame of mind" for the part. Above all, he strongly believed in the film. Susie Hinton speaks of Dillon with great emotion: "Matt identified with Rusty. . . . He is exactly the kind of kid I write about. Of course, he is more complex than my characters, but he has the same traits as they do. He also possesses the same charming arrogance as Rusty James."

Fred Roos is the one to be congratulated for his selection of Mickey Rourke for the part of the Motorcycle Boy. Rourke auditioned for *The Outsiders* and both Roos and Coppola were greatly impressed by him. Unfortunately, there was no part for Rourke in *The Outsiders.* But as soon as Coppola had "fallen in love" with *Rumble Fish,* he contacted Rourke. "It's going to be super," said Roos. "I am really pleased to have introduced him [Mickey Rourke] to Francis. They hit it off right away." Mickey Rourke is an unusual actor. He had appeared previously in *Body Heat* as the young pyromaniac. His performance in *Rumble Fish* revealed his talent. He was one of the great acting discoveries of recent years. Rourke has this uncanny ability to make the audience strain to listen to his nearly whispered monologues, despite all of the noise in the background. And that half-smile . . .

Rourke compared the character of the Motorcycle Boy to that of "an actor who no longer finds his work interesting: it is no longer what it used to be. It's just garbage. . . . And there is no way out. And no one listens to anyone else. . . . The [character of the] mother is an extension of the Motorcycle Boy. Because everyone wants to be free."

Dennis Hopper, another exceptional actor and a friend of Coppola's, portrayed the father of the two boys. He had already appeared in *Apocalypse Now* as the photographer. Rourke spoke highly of him: "You react to him even when he is off camera. He helped us. Whenever Francis wanted something from me, he would tell Dennis. Then he would get it."

Diane Lane played the part of Rusty James's girlfriend, Cherry, and Nicolas Cage, nephew of the "boss," played Smokey. Tom Waits, another familiar figure by now, appeared as Benny, the owner of the coffee shop.

When the film was presented at the New York Film Festival in October 1983, the audience, made up primarily of critics, booed. "There is a New York snobbishness. . . . Not a single person spoke of the positive aspects of the film—the actors' performances, the aesthetic research. . . . No. The critics just insulted me," said Coppola, more disillusioned than ever before. Less than one month after its release, only one theater in New York was showing *Rumble Fish*. And it was empty. Who said critics have no influence?

Voyage to the End of the Night

If *The Outsiders* was a blueprint—in Technicolor—of a story about teenagers, *Rumble Fish* was its negative. The sharp black-and-white contrasts were violent, baroque, and sometimes difficult to sustain. Any romanticism that

The inimitable gaze of Mickey Rourke.

could be found in *The Outsiders* had disappeared entirely in *Rumble Fish*. The universe of *Rumble Fish* is a desperate one, reminiscent of those of Carson McCullers and Tennessee Williams.

In a town removed from time, life is a relentless attempt at survival, often resulting in self-destruction. Rather than a class struggle, it is a life struggle.

The film's metaphor is an exotic fish that wages deadly wars against its own kind—even against its own reflection. Despair reigns in these streets. The flamboyance of those Oklahoma sunsets are equaled by the dismal gloominess of this nameless city.

The Outsiders spoke of the courage to live. *Rumble Fish* whispers about the very absurdity of life. Coppola's references to Camus were not coincidental!

But *Rumble Fish* is above all the story of two brothers, of Rusty James's untiring admiration for the Motorcycle Boy. When the Motorcycle Boy returns from his California quest, he knows there is no way out of the nightmare.

Nearly deaf—as a result of all those fights—he longer wants to hear what goes on around him; color-blind, he cannot see what is "over the rainbow." Only the purity (the "gold") of childhood could save him. But it is too late; time has dug the grave, and dreams and illusions have long been buried.

The Motorcycle Boy is living his final reprieve. Rusty James does not realize this, because he is younger and still credulous. He admires his older brother and tries to understand the reasons for his inconsolable disenchantment.

The clouds go by at full speed, reflected in a windowpane. They announce the drama that will follow. "Time is a funny thing," says the man in the coffee shop.

Rumble Fish is a film about time. The time of life. How much time is left? As an omen of imminent death, we see a clock without any hands. Yes, time is a funny thing.

The Motorcycle Boy identifies with the rumble fish. Like him, they are prisoners. To each his hell—or his fishbowl.

He wants to return the fish to their original habitat, the river. He breaks down the door to the pet shop, opens all the cages, and seizes his "aquatic brothers." But law and order interfere with his plans. The "jailers" do not sleep at night, they would rather kill. The Motorcycle Boy will be shot as he is making his desperate escape. But he did manage to get his message through to Rusty James, who will take the fish to the river . . .

"I wish I were the big brother you always wanted," the Motorcycle Boy had said to Rusty James. Rusty James is now a big boy himself. Freed from his hero worship, and alone, he begins to realize that "the heart is a lonely hunter."

Rumble Fish is a tribute to August Coppola, Francis's older brother, "my

A graffito never seen in *Rumble Fish*. This scene was cut from the final version.

The film's metaphor: the rumble fish.

first and best teacher." This is of great importance to Coppola: "My brother is five years older than I and he was my idol. He was very good to me. He took me absolutely everywhere and taught me everything. He was the leader of a group. He was very handsome and still is. And he could have easily pushed me away or told me to leave him alone. I slept in the same room with him until I was eleven years old."

Rumble Fish is a baffling film, a brilliant gem of black gold, shining like the blade of a knife in the reflection of a streetlamp. And it is us that Coppola slashes. We cannot leave as we entered. We have been wounded. Fatally.

**Eddy Malloy leading the Mills Blue
Rhythm Band at the Cotton Club.**

11 When Harlem Was in Vogue

The Cotton Club

In the fall of 1982, following the completion of the surrealistic marvel that was *Rumble Fish,* Coppola, who was emotionally exhausted, considered a temporary retirement from the film milieu. But in January of 1983, Coppola was offered the job of directing *The Pope of Greenwich Village,* with Al Pacino and Mickey Rourke. (Eric Roberts and Mickey Rourke ultimately appeared in the film.) Francis regained his enthusiasm after reading the screenplay of this phychological drama about small-time Mafiosi. "I had several good ideas on the subject, I had Vittorio Storaro and the desire to make a murky film in the style of George Orwell and set in New York City. I was very excited about it. But the producers began postponing it, partly because of Al Pacino, who was still shooting another film. And the project was indefinitely halted."

Besides the artistic interest that this film offered the Wonder Boy, the screenplay would enable Coppola to help the financially troubled Zoetrope Studios (to this day, Coppola is still in debt for millions of dollars as a result of the financially catastrophic undertaking *One from the Heart*). But now he was forced to wait until February, then March. Rather than mope about, Coppola returned to his Napa Valley home to work on another project he had been considering for a long time. In two months, he had written nearly four hundred pages.

During this very creative time, Coppola received a phone call from Robert Evans. His only previous contact with the producer had taken place during the production of *The Godfather,* "Bob encourages people to take care of him. Perhaps because he looks like a headstrong prince. . . . In any event, he found himself in trouble several times, and I always felt obliged to help him. This time, he was desperate. He used a strange metaphor about 'his baby being ill and needing a doctor.' What he was refering to was the screenplay of *The Cotton Club,* written by Mario Puzo: Evans did not know where to begin with it, so he called Coppola. Coppola replied that he would be happy to help out for a week or two, offering graciously to give his opinion and a few suggestions.

Evans arrived with the screenplay. Coppola realized right away that nothing could be accomplished in one week: "There was nothing there, it was a futile gangster story devoid of any zest."

So Coppola began doing some research. The heyday of the Cotton Club was during the years 1925–1928. It was a lively time, a rich, stimulating period when Harlem was the residential area for well-to-do blacks. The Cotton Club attracted a top-notch audience: F. Scott Fitzgerald, Charlie Chaplin, Cole Porter, but also Al Capone . . . Lady Mountbatten refered to the Cotton Club as "the aristocrat of Harlem." What made the cabaret singular was that the audience was exclusively white while the performers and the staff were black. There were occasional exceptions, as for the boxer Jack Johnson. And the music, the music was marvelous—Cab Calloway and Duke Ellington!

Coppola's research aroused his interest. He rewrote the screenplay in collaboration with William Kennedy, the author of the Albany trilogy *Legs, Billy Phelan's Greatest Game,* and *Ironweed.*

The result was effective. Evans was so enthralled by this new screenplay that he asked Coppola to direct it (originally, Evans was going to direct it himself). But Coppola refused, "because I was terrified of being in a position where other people control what I do. Because my ideas don't gel when I first describe them, but when I can work them out myself, they always turn out well." The fear of having to fight for each concept for the film, as he had, day after day, during the filming of *The Godfather,* discouraged Coppola from the very start. Hence the ultimatum he delivered to Evans: full control of the production or no go. Evans accepted.

Coppola knew that the only way to recapture the feeling of another time was to show it through its men and women. He would portray their habits, their desires, what made their hearts beat faster, the things for which they were prepared to kill or die. Coppola had already accomplished this several times, recreating the past and the present in feverish and animated chronicles whose protagonists make up the fabric of America. For all of America is contained in Coppola, from the "Godfathers" of the Mafia, to the soldiers of *Apocalypse Now* caught in a nightmare, to the lost adolescents of *Rumble Fish* and *The Outsiders*.

"Everyone wants to know," says Coppola with false surprise, "if *Cotton Club* is a gangster film or a musical." The answer is simple: *Cotton Club* is both—and more. It is also a commentary on cinema itself.

The Cotton Club is a "mirror" which reflects the images of films that have been made before, such as the Warner films of the 1930s, including musicals like *Forty-Second Street* and the *Golddiggers* films, and gangster films like *Public Enemy*.

"And yet, everything in this film is true," says Coppola cunningly. "Certain things may have been manipulated or rearranged, but there is no one incident or anecdote which is not a true one."

The film tells the story of the jazz era, of prohibition in Harlem in the early 1930s. As in François Truffaut's *The Last Metro,* where the theater gave us "behind-the-scenes" access, both figuratively and literally, to the German Occupation, the Cotton Club becomes the place where individuals come to terms with their destinies. The Cotton Club becomes the microcosm of a time and place.

Left, top: **The entrance to the real Cotton Club in 1930.**

Left, middle: **Several members of the Cotton Club orchestra in the early 1930s.**

Left, bottom: **The club's program in the fall of 1933.**

Harlem Nights

From the very first images that follow the dazzling opening credits, we are caught up in the life of the Cotton Club, located at the intersection of Lenox Avenue and 142nd Street. Black chorus girls are dancing to the wild music of Duke Ellington. Since 1927, Duke Ellington and his orchestra had been bringing the house down with musical numbers such as "Cotton Club Stomp," "Creole Love Call," "East St. Louis Toodle-oo," "Minnie the Moocher," "Black Beauty," "Mood Indigo," and many more. Coppola reinstates the look and the sound of that time as it has never been done before. He uses the raw and sensual sounds, as golden as the skin of the dancers and musicians who performed them.

While all the artists and waiters of the Cotton Club were black, the audience was exclusively white. There are some white people backstage as well—the owner of the club, Owney Madden, a bootlegger and gang leader, and his bodyguard and righthand man, who spreads fear among the performers. The nighttime world of excitement is represented by the blacks, while daylight and corruption are symbolized by the whites.

Sandman Williams (Gregory Hines) goes to see a black gangster, asking for his help and advice. The gangster tells Sandman that "for the time being, we must accept the laws of the Jews, the Irish, and the Italians. We are not yet strong enough to challenge them." To which Sandman replies: "Then I will have to tap-dance my way to revenge." This could be one of the morals of the film—"a film about servitude," adds Coppola. While the show goes on, with all of its glitter and

Opposite page: **A rehearsal at the Cotton Club in 1930. Sonny Greer on percussion.**

rhythmic music, a violent subplot is unfolding. As a background theme, the gang war escalates, each faction trying to dominate the alcohol bootlegging trade. We are in the midst of prohibition, which would lead to great thirsts for power and inevitable bloodbaths among criminals. To the sound of tap dancing and mellow brass, death lurks about, bringing together, if only for a short time, entertainers and killers, show business and scum. As always in Coppola's films, one can hear the dirge of a crumbling society, of a world tottering on its foundations. No one can match Coppola's ability to show the flaws in a social structure and the headiness of those who have reached the top by means of crime and corruption.

Besides Sandman Williams, other characters are featured against this violent background. There are Sandman's friend Lila Rose (Lonette McKee), a light-skinned dancer and singer, Dixie Dwyer (Richard Gere), a white trumpet player, and his mistress, Vera Cicero (Diane Lane)—and, moving all around them, an entire group of small-time hoods and bigtime gangsters.

In the late 1920s, prohibition has given rise to an incredible proliferation of crime and violence throughout the United States. In New York, many speakeasies and nightclubs are supplied with bootlegged alcohol distributed by gangs who are constantly defending their territory from rivals. Harlem's chic quarter vibrates to the hot tempo of jazz, and in the Cotton Club, Harlem's most famous night spot, politicians, gangsters, and stars sit side by side. Caught up in the fever of the Roaring Twenties, several small-timers try their luck at making a better life for themselves. Two black brothers, Sandman and Clay Williams, both tap dancers, audition at the Cotton Club. Sandman is entranced by Lila Rose, a light-skinned entertainer he sees at the club.

In another nightclub, Dixie Dwyer, a white trumpet player, is having a jam session with some of his friends. Dutch Schultz, a bootlegger, is impressed by the performer's style. Vera Cicero, Dutch's girlfriend, falls for the musician's charm. Suddenly, a rival gang bursts on the scene and begins shooting. With a miraculous move, Dixie saves Dutch from being killed. To thank Dixie, Dutch hires him on the spot. One of his responsibilities will be to look after Vera. As he takes her home, Dixie resists her advances.

Meanwhile, Sandman Williams is hired at the Cotton Club, but without his brother. His ensuing success causes him to drift farther and farther away from his brother. When not performing, Sandman looks for any excuse to talk to Lila and declare his love. But the opportunities are slim and the young woman's attitude toward him is anything but friendly.

All of the artists, who are black, are constantly mistreated by club owner Owney Madden's watchdog, who one day actually threatens Sandman's life. Lila, who has witnessed the scene, is overwhelmed by the event, which she sees as the symbol of an unacceptable situation. She decides to leave the club, making Sandman terribly sad.

In an effort to cut down on gang wars, Dutch Schultz agrees to meet with his arch-rival, Joe Flynn, "the Irishman." But a violent fight ensues, resulting in Flynn's death, which is witnessed by Dixie and Vera. In spite of his disgust, Dixie realizes he can never leave Dutch. What's more, Dixie has fallen in love with Vera and has become her lover. Dutch senses the electricity between Vera and Dixie: jealous, he sends Dixie to Hollywood. There, Dixie makes a film and gains celebrity, but soon returns to New York. Dutch has given Vera a nightclub which has become very popular and which features Lila Rose. One day, Sandman decides to visit her there, but he cannot get in, for, as in the Cotton Club, the audience is strictly white. Forced to go out in the street to see Sandman, Lila falls into his arms. Sandman tries to convince Lila to return to the Cotton Club (even though he hates the club and wants revenge), but she refuses. Lila and Sandman will eventually marry.

In a parallel vein, Vincent Dwyer, Dixie's younger brother, dreams of becoming rich. To this purpose, he works for Schultz, setting up bootlegging rackets in several bars and restaurants in New York City. When Dixie learns of his brother's activities, he pleads with him to stop before it is too late, but his brother persists. The violence escalates, culminating in a bloody incident that claims the lives of five innocent children. This event causes such intense repercussions that the Mob decides to eliminate Vincent. His life in danger, and needing money to get out of town, Vincent kidnaps Frenchy, Owney Madden's righthand man. Dixie becomes the intermediary who will deliver the ransom money to his brother and free Frenchy. But Dixie's worst fears are confirmed: Vincent is shot down right after the exchange is completed.

Dutch Schultz is killed soon thereafter in a quiet little restaurant. Such is the law of the jungle. At the same moment, Sandman performs a triumphal dance sequence under Lila's loving gaze. The film's epilogue thus fluctuates between scintillating nightlife and harsh reality. On the stage of the Cotton Club, the performers act out the departure of the two couples. Dixie is about to leave town alone by train when he sees Vera waiting for him on the platform with her luggage. Sandman and Lila, newlyweds, exult in happiness. These four have found peace now that they are free of corruption and tyranny. . . .

Coppola turned a "simple gangster film," as he himself called it, into a powerful saga.

Using the cliché as a semantic basis for his film, Coppola removed any surprise from the subject: he knows that we already know all there is to know about the time in question. Rather than tell it to us again, he mimes it, constructing a drama that is pure cinema. The audience can either give in to the fireworks of shattered glass or avoid its dangerous slivers. When the visual saturation point is nearly reached, Coppola switches to the medium of sound. This is the culmination of what was begun in *The Conversation*. Thus the almost elliptic depiction of the murder of Dutch and his men finds its true violence in the unrestrained tap-dance sequence that takes place in the Cotton Club. The lap dissolve is reinvented here for both sound and image. The resulting effect is that of a naturalist and expressionist fresco.

The dance floor of the Cotton Club reflects the advent of modern jazz and big-time crime. Musicians and thugs alike shift uncomfortably under the ruthless gaze of Lucky Luciano, who has now stepped into a position of power. The dance floor also represents the daily tragedy of the individual trapped within his skin color, sex, or social class. These short, tight sequences are skillfully dispersed throughout the film, to the convulsive beat of jazz. The symmetry of the white/black couples (Dixie-Vera and Sandman-Lila) is repeated in the symmetry of triumphs and downfalls, black skin and white skin, backstage and back alleys, flashes of stagelights and splashes of blood. The musical numbers are orchestrated like criminal operations and the gang fights are choreographed with the precision of dance sequences. In his own way, Coppola pays tribute to the director of *Mean Streets* and *New York, New York,* Martin Scorsese—Coppola works Scorsese's territory with less intuition but more intelligence, less lyricism but more sensuality.

For despite its apparent intellectualism, *The Cotton Club* captures the heart. Tenderness is a great leveler. "As he did in *The Rain People*, Coppola captures his characters' bouts with the blues," writes Francis Forestier in *L'Express*. "As he did in *The Godfather*, he recounts a bloody urban saga. As he did in *The Conversation*, he makes sound dominate imagery. As he did in *Apocalypse Now*, by his staging he mitigates the madness of the shooting."

To recreate this American microcosm, Coppola seems to have taken Jean Renoir's advice: to fill the canvas completely, at any cost. Without the slightest trace of gratuitous virtuosity, Coppola delivers a kaleidoscope of continuous visual pleasure, a result of impressively fluid and elegant editing.

By combining composite elements, Coppola performs a majestic synthesis that takes the form of a dazzling show. Not just a musical set in a gangster milieu, but a veritable requiem.

The hardships of life fill *The Cotton Club,* and yet, the film's ending is a happy one. The Cotton Club performers mime Dixie and Vera's departure on board the Twentieth Century Limited. And from their platform, the camera travels to a real platform where the film's main characters, who have finally found their freedom, will meet again. Coppola shares a moment of complicity with his peers: the film's final scene is as elegant as the ending of Jean Renoir's *The Golden Coach,* as impetuous as Bob Fosse's *All That Jazz,* as impertinent as Fellini's *8½.* But the film is beautiful because it is pure Coppola.

12   The Last Tycoon

"You can count them on the fingers of one hand, those men who can find the equation of the film world," writes F. Scott Fitzgerald in *The Last Tycoon*. Such men no longer exist. After their long reign in Hollywood, they have disappeared forever, leaving behind their deserted studios that still echo with the memories of their extravagant excesses.

What remains today is the flashiness of a Tinsel Town that is dominated by the television industry: fast productions intended for even faster consumption.

"It is a story of another time," Fitzgerald wrote. A time whose memory fades day by day.

Coppola has also abandoned his studio. Zoetrope has returned to its beginnings on Kearny Street in San Francisco. And this without too much regret, as at the end of a great adventure of which one wishes to remember only the best times. "We were very young, and very sincere, and we thought ourselves to be the American filmmakers of tomorrow, and Zoetrope symbolized traditional cinema," remembers Coppola with a touch of nostalgia. What else could we think?

The enthusiasm of the early days has been dulled. There had been a dream of bringing back to life an old-fashioned Hollywood studio. Zoetrope will, once again, change its

name: to Zoetrope Corporation perhaps, taken over by Chrysler . . . But nothing is certain yet.

Has Hollywood forgiven this "bad boy" for refusing to play its impossible game? Hollywood is too enamored of success to tolerate the imposing of new rules. Coppola went too far, perhaps, but his was not a total loss. He is wiser now, ready for a temporary and restorative exile.

The days of startling declarations are over, as are the insolent defiance, the careless spending of staggering sums of money, and the megalomania. No more putting everything on the line for each new undertaking, each new gamble, each one more risky than the one that preceeded it. Coppola realizes this quite well: "The film establishment will not tolerate me any further." Coppola has not forgotten the critics, who have become increasingly harsh, refusing, at least in the United States, to give him the freedom to make experimental films. Something went wrong between Coppola and the critics, "a reciprocal misunderstanding that cannot be corrected." They failed to recognize Coppola's fundamental sincerity, they tired of his cavalier and defiant attitude. And in the future, Coppola hopes to avoid them altogether. "Adults no longer interest me," he likes to say, "I don't wish to have anything to do with them."

"In order to succeed, you must be hated," Coppola once proclaimed in

1974. From that viewpoint, he certainly did succeed. Ever since the release of *The Conversation* and *The Godfather, Part II,* his films have met with bad reviews and financial failure. One cannot help but think of other "exiled" film directors who made films that defied the norm: Chaplin, Welles, Mankiewicz.

Will it takes years then for Hollywood to finally accept Coppola as one of their own? It might be too late by then, for Coppola is quite serious about retirement, at least temporarily. "The industry, and film people, all bore me tremendously," repeats Coppola, "and I intend to remove myself from that environment because it no longer appeals to me. It is not a place for a guy like me."

The man who is speaking is at midlife, at the age of forty-five. He has reached the end of the second stage of his career. Ten years earlier, as he began working on the production of *Apocalypse Now,* he had reached the end of the first part. This is a privileged moment, a time to take stock. Childhood is a sweet memory, perhaps the best time of his life. "What interests me now is to see that the young receive a good legacy from the cinema and to see that they have the freedom to take it even further." In his particular case, the succession is assured. His name will not disappear from the big screen. Gian Carlo, his eldest son, is ready. And Zoetrope is in possession of the rights to several important projects: *Peter Pan,* and Jack Kerouac's *On the Road,* among others.

Plans are already in the works for Gian Carlo, alone, to do the adaptation of Kerouac's novel, using his father's electronically equipped video trailer. Like his father, fifteen years earlier in *The Rain People,* Gian Carlo will also be "on the road," as the film will undoubtedly be a "road movie."

Coppola, casting a watchful glance over his brood (his younger son Roman also works with him), will be able to devote himself to the "big project" he has envisioned for many years. It will be something "devastating," he promises. "I would like to change my qualifications, to become a kind of chromatic novelist. I want to be inspired not by the great film directors but by the great novelists and philosophers, the very ones who were the main interest of my brother August: Joyce, Thomas Mann, etc. I would like to write a novel, using the material I expect to gather, but rather than write a book, I would do it in 'film writing.'" He has already written four hundred pages, a rough draft of something entitled *Megalopolis,* which will be a study of contemporary thought and set in New York. This "film" would examine such essential questions as: Who are we? Where do we come from? What will happen to the human race? As in Joyce's *Ulysses,* the action will take place in one day and will involve numerous characters. But Coppola also speaks of "a part that takes place in Ancient Rome, right before Caesar, when the world was obsessed with death and money. A society in the height of decadence.

"I want to make an epic film about our times, a film that speaks of utopia. We will live to see the utopia we have been mocking all along. And yet the root of the word means 'nowhere.' We don't think enough about this phenomenon." Coppola is already planning techniques that are even more experimental than his past ones. The film's distribution will be handled in the 'usual' manner, but the production will be accomplished twenty times faster. At the same cost, the result will be twenty times more effective . . . "Film as we know it today is doomed," explains Coppola, "there are no more full-length black-and-white, 35-millimeter features. Film is a carriage without a horse. But history has taught us that this type of innovation cannot be stopped. And this one will revolutionize the world. Politics, economy, the arts . . . and I hope it will improve them. I am waiting for that new world and I am preparing for it, as it will be the world of my old age and I have lost faith in the world of today."

Like Monroe Stahr in *The Last Tycoon,* Coppola has "long since wandered into unexplored regions of perception where very few [can] follow him."

Filmography

TONIGHT FOR SURE

U.S.A., 1961.
Produced by: Francis Coppola.
Length: 75 minutes.
Black and white.
Screenplay: Jerry Shaffer and Francis Coppola.
Director: Francis Coppola.
Director of Photography: Jack Hill.
Editor: Ronald Walter.
Music: Carmine Coppola.
Art Director: Albert Locatelli.

DEMENTIA 13

U.S.A., Filmgroup, 1963.
English title: The Haunted and the Hunted.
Produced by: Roger Corman for Warner Bros.
Length: 81 minutes.
Black and white.
Screenplay: Francis Ford Coppola.
Director: Francis Ford Coppola.
Assistant Director: Richard Dalton.
Director of Photography: Charles Hannawalt.
Art Director: Albert Locatelli.
Set Designer: Eleonor Neil.
Music: Ronald Stein.
Editor: Stewart O'Brien.
Cast: William Campbell (Richard Holoran), Luana Anders (Louise), Bart Patton (Billy Holoran), Mary Mitchell (Kane), Patrick Magee (Justin Caleb), Peter Reed (John Holoran).
Premiere: September 25, 1963, in Los Angeles.

YOU'RE A BIG BOY NOW

U.S.A., 1966.
Produced by: Seven Arts for Warner Bros.
Length: 96 minutes.
Technicolor.
Screenplay: Francis Ford Coppola, from the novel by David Benedictus.
Director: Francis Ford Coppola.
Director of Photography: Andy Laszlo.
Editor: Aram Avakian.
Music: Bob Prince; songs by John Sebastian.
Art Director: Vassele Fotopoulos.
Costume Design: Theoni V. Aldredge.
Cast: Peter Kastner (Bernard Chanticleer), Elizabeth Hartman (Barbara Darling), Geraldine Page (Margery Chanticleer), Julie Harris (Miss Thing), Rip Torn (I. H. Chanticleer), Karen Black (Amy), Michael De Dunn (Richard Mudd), Doplh Sweet (Francis Graf), Michael O'Sullivan (Kurt Doughty).
Premiere: December 9, 1966, in Los Angeles.

FINIAN'S RAINBOW

U.S.A., 1968.
Produced by: Joseph Landon for Warner Bros.
Length: 114 minutes.
Technicolor, Panavision, 70-mm.
Screenplay: E. Y. Harburg and Fred Saidy.
Music: Burton J. Lane.
Lyrics: E. Y. Harburg
Director: Francis Coppola.
Photography: Philip Lathrop.
Editor: Melvin Shapiro.
Choreography: Hermes Pan.
Cast: Fred Astaire (Finian McLonergan), Petula Clark (Sharon), Tommy Steele (Og), Don Francks (Woody), Keenan Wynn (Senator Hawkins).
Premiere: October 9, 1968, in New York.

THE RAIN PEOPLE

U.S.A., 1969.
Produced by: Bart Patton and Ronald Colby for Warner Bros.
Length: 102 minutes.
Technicolor.
Screenplay and direction: Francis Ford Coppola.
Director of Photography: Wilmer Butler.
Art Director: Leon Erickson.
Music: Ronald Stein and Carmine Coppola.
Sound: Walter Murch and Nathan Boxer.
Editor: Blackie Malkin.
Cast: James Caan (Jimmy Kilgannon), Shirley Knight (Natalie Ravenna), Robert Duvall (Gordon), Marya Zimmet (Rosalie), Tom Aldredge (Mr. Alfred), Laurie Crews (Ellen), Andrew Duncan (Artie), Margaret Fairchild (Marion), Sally Gracie (Beth), Alan Manson (Lou), Robert Modica (Vinny).
Premiere: August 27, 1969, in New York.
Awarded the grand prizes at the 1969 international festival at San Sebastian, for Best Film and Best Director.

THE GODFATHER

U.S.A., 1972.
Produced by: Albert S. Ruddy for Paramount.
Length: 175 minutes.
Technicolor.
Screenplay: Mario Puzo and Francis Ford Coppola, from the novel by Mario Puzo.
Director: Francis Ford Coppola.
Director of Photography: Gordon Willis.
Editors: William Reynolds, Peter Zinner, Marc Laub, Murray Solomon.
Production Designer: Dean Tavoularis.
Art Director: Wärren Clynner.
Music: Nino Rota.
Costume Design: Anna Hill Johnstone.
Cast: Marlon Brando (Don Vito Corleone), Al Pacino (Michael Corleone), James Caan (Sonny Corleone), Richard Castellano (Clemenza), Robert Duvall (Tom Hagen), Sterling Hayden (McClumskey), John Marley (Jack Woltz), Richard Conte (Barzini), Diane Keaton (Kay Adams), Al Littieri (Sollozzo), Abe Vigoda (Tessio), Talia Shire (Connie Rizzi), Johnny Russo (Carlo Rizzi), John Cazale (Freddie Corleone), Rudy Bond (Cuneo), Al Martino (Johnny Fontane), Morgana King (Mama Corleone), Lenny Montana (Luca Brasi), John Martino (Paulie Gatto), Salvatore Corsitto (Bonasera), Richard Wright (Neri), Alex Rocco (Moe Greene), Tony Giorgio (Bruno Tattaglia), Vito Scottia (Nazorine), Tere Livrano (Theresa Hagen), Victor Rendina (Philip Tattaglia), Jeannie Linero (Lucy Mancini), Julie Gregg (Sandra Corleone), Ardell Sheridan (Mrs. Clemenza), Simonetta Stefanelli (Appolonia), Angelo Infanti (Fabrizio), Corrado Gaipa (Don Tommasino), Franco Citti (Calo), Saro Urzi (Vitelli).
Premiere: March 11, 1972 in New York.
Oscars were awarded for Best Film, Best Actor (Marlon Brando), and Best Screenplay (adaptation).

THE CONVERSATION

U.S.A., 1974
Produced by: Fred Roos and Francis Coppola (Coppola Company) for Paramount.
Length: 113 minutes.
Technicolor.
Screenplay and direction: Francis Ford Coppola.
Director of Photography: Bill Butler.
Editing and Sound: Walter Murch.
Editing and Sound Assistant: Richard Chew.
Music: David Shire.
Production Design: Dean Tavoularis.
Technical Advisers: Hal Lipset and Leo Jones.
Cast: Gene Hackman (Harry Caul), John Cazale (Stan), Allen Garfield (Bernie Moran), Frederic Forrest (Mark), Cindy Williams (Ann), Michael Higgins (Paul), Elizabeth MacRae (Meredith), Teri Garr (Amy), Harrison Ford (Martin Stett), Mark Wheeler (the receptionist), Robert Shields (the mime), Phoebe Alexander (Lurleen).
Premiere: April 7, 1974, in New York.
Awarded the Palme d'Or at the 1974 Cannes International Film Festival.

THE GODFATHER, PART II

U.S.A., 1974.
Produced by: Francis Coppola, Fred Roos, and Gray Frederikson (Coppola Company) for Paramount.
Length: 220 minutes.
Technicolor.
Screenplay: Francis Coppola and Mario Puzo, from the novel by Mario Puzo.
Director: Francis Coppola.
Director of Photography: Gordon Willis.
Editing: Peter Zinner, Barry Malkin, Richard Marks.
Production Designer: Dean Tavoularis.
Set Decoration: George R. Nelson.
Music: Nino Rota and Carmine Coppola.
Costume Designer: Theodora Van Rumkle.
Cast: Al Pacino (Michael Corleone), Robert Duval (Tom Hagen), Diane Keaton (Kay Adams Corleone), Robert de Niro (Vito Corleone), John Cazale (Freddie Corleone), Talia Shire (Connie Corleone), Lee Strasberg (Hyman Roth), Michael V. Gazzo (Frankie Pentangeli), G. D. Spradin (Sena-

tor Pat Geary), Richard Bright (Al Neri), Gaston Moschin (Fanucci), Tom Rosqui (Rocco Lampone), B. Kearby, Jr. (young Clemenza), Frank Sivero (Genco), Francesca de Sapio (young Mama Corleone), Morgana King (Mama Corleone), Mariana Hill (Deanna Corleone), Leopoldo Trieste (Signor Roberto), Dominic Chianese (Johnny Ola), Amerigo Tot (Michael's bodyguard), Troy Donahue (Merle Johnson), John Aprea (young Tessio), Joe Spinell (Willi Cicci), Abe Vigoda (Tessio), Tere Livrano (Theresa Hagen), Gianni Russo (Carlo Rizzi), Maria Carta (Vito's mother), Oreste Baldini (Vito Andolini as a boy), Giuseppe Sillato (Don Francesco), Mario Cotone (Don Tommasino), James Gournaris (Anthony Corleone), Fay Spain (Mrs. Marcia Roth), Harry Dean Stanton (FBI agent), David Baker (second FBI agent), Carmine Caridi (Carmine Rosato), Danny Aiello (Tony Rosato), Carmine Foresta (a policeman), Nick Discenza (bartender), Father Joseph Medeglia (Father Carmelo), William Bowers (the chairman of the committee), Ezio Flagello (agent), Livio Giorgio (tenor in Sneza Mamma), Kathy Beller (the girl in Sneza Mamma), Saveria Mazzola (Signora Colombo), Tita Alban (Cuban president), Johnny Naranjo (the Cuban interpreter), Elda Maida (Frank's wife), Salvatore Po (Pentangeli's brother), Ignazio Pappalardo (Mosca), Andrea Maugeri (Strollo), Peter La Corte (Signor Abbandando), Vincent Coppola (salesman), Peter Donat (Questadt), Tom Dahlgren (Fred Corngold), Paul B. Brown (Senator Reams), Yvonne Coll (Yolanda), J. D. Nichols (brothel manager), Edward Van Sickle (Ellis Island doctor), Gabria Belloni (Ellis Island nurse), Richard Watson (customs officer), Venancia Grangerard (Cuban nurse), Erica Yohn (governess), Theresa Tirelli (midwife), James Caan (Sonny Corleone).
Premiere: December 12, 1974, in New York.
Oscars for Best Film, Best Supporting Actor (Robert de Niro), Best Director, Best Screenplay (adaptation), Best Set Design (Dean Tavoularis, Angelo Graham, and George Nelson), and Best Original Musical Score (Nino Rota and Carmine Coppola).

APOCALYPSE NOW

U.S.A., 1979.
Produced by: Francis Coppola, Fred Roos, Gray Frederikson, and Tom Sternberg (Omni Zoetrope) for Zoetrope Studios.

Length: 146 minutes (70-mm), 153 minutes (35-mm).
Technicolor.
Screenplay: Francis Coppola and John Milius.
Director of Photography: Vittorio Storaro.
Production Designer: Dean Tavoularis.
Sound and Sound Editing: Walter Murch.
Editors: Walter Murch, Gerald B. Greenberg, and Lisa Fruchtman.
Music: Carmine Coppola and Francis Coppola.
Special effects: Larry Cavanaugh, Jerry Endler, Rudy Liszczak, John Fraser, Richard Helmer, Ted Martin, Eddie Ayay, David St. Ana, Mario Carmona.
Cast: Marlon Brando (Colonel Kurtz), Martin Sheen (Captain Benjamin Willard), Robert Duvall (Lieutenant Colonel Kilgore), Frederic Forrest (Chef), Albert Hall (Chief), Sam Bottoms (Lance), Larry Fishburne (Clean), Dennis Hopper (photographer), G. D. Spradlin (the general), Harrison Ford (the colonel), Jerry Ziesner (civilian), Scott Glenn (Colby), Bo Byers (MP first sergeant), James Kean (Kilgore's machine-gunner), Kerry Rossall (Mike, from San Diego), Ron McQueen (wounded soldier), Tom Mason (Sergeant Fourier), Cynthia Wood (playmate of the year), Colleen Camp (playmate), Linda Carpenter (playmate), Jack Thibeau (soldier wearing raincoat), Glenn Walken (Lieutenant Carlsen), George Cantero (soldier with suitcase), Damian Leake (gunner), Herb Rice (Roach).
Premiere: September 26, 1979, in Paris.
Awarded the Palme D'Or (in a tie with Volker Schlöndorff's *The Tin Drum*) at the 1979 Cannes Film Festival.
Oscars for Best Photography (Vittorio Storaro) and Best Sound (Walter Murch, Mark Berger, Richard Beggs, and Nat Boxer).

ONE FROM THE HEART

U.S.A., 1982.
Produced by: Fred Roos and Gray Frederikson for Zoetrope Studios.
Assistant producers: Teri Fettis and Dan Suhart.
Length: 107 minutes.
Technicolor.
Screenplay: Armyan Bernstein and Francis Coppola.
Director: Francis Coppola.
Director of Photography: Vittorio Storaro.
Production Designer: Dean Tavoularis.
Music and Lyrics: Tom Waits.

Songs performed by: Crystal Gayle and Tom Waits.
Costume Designer: Ruth Morley.
Editing: Anne Goursaud, with Rudi Fehr and Randy Roberts.
Special Visual Effects: Robert Swarthe.
Cast: Frederic Forrest (Hank), Teri Garr (Franny), Raul Julia (Ray), Nastassia Kinski (Leila), Lainie Kazan (Maggie), Harry Dean Stanton (Moe), Allen Goorwitz (restaurant owner), Italia and Carmine Coppola (the couple in the elevator).
Premiere: Spring 1982 in the United States.

THE OUTSIDERS

U.S.A., 1982.
Produced by: Fred Roos and Gray Frederikson for Zoetrope Studios.
Length: 91 minutes.
Technicolor.
Screenplay: Kathleen Knutsen Rowell, from the novel by S. E. Hinton.
Director: Francis Coppola.
Director of Photography: Stephen Burum.
Production Engineer: Dean Tavoularis.
Music: Carmine Coppola.
Opening song performed by: Stevie Wonder.
Editor: Anne Goursaud.
Cast: C. Thomas Howell (Ponyboy), Matt Dillon (Dallas), Ralph Macchio (Johnny), Rob Lowe (Sodapop), Patrick Swayze (Darrel), Emilio Estevez (Two-Bit), Diane Lane (Cherry), Leif Garrett (Bob), Darren Dalton (Randy), S. E. Hinton (the nurse).
Premiere: March 25, 1983, in the United States.

RUMBLE FISH

U.S.A., 1982.
Produced by: Fred Roos and Doug Claybourne for Zoetrope Studios.
Length: 94 minutes.
Black and white and Technicolor.
Screenplay: S. E. Hinton and Francis Coppola, based on the novel by S. E. Hinton.
Director: Francis Ford Coppola.
Director of Photography: Stephen Burum.
Production Designer: Dean Tavoularis.
Music: Stewart Copeland.
Editor: Anne Goursaud.
Cast: Matt Dillon (Rusty James), Mickey Rourke (Motorcycle Boy), Diane Lane (Patty), Dennis Hopper (the father), Vincent Spano (Steve), Nicholas Cage (Smokey), Diana Scarwid (Cassandra), Tom Waits (Benny), Doimino (Patty's sister), S. E. Hinton (the prostitute in the street), Glenn Withrow (Biff).

Premiere: October 9, 1983, in New York (New York Film Festival).

THE COTTON CLUB

U.S.A., 1983.
Produced by: Robert Evans for Totally Independent Limited.
Length: 128 minutes.
Technicolor.
Screenplay: Francis Coppola and William Kennedy, based on Jim Haskins's *The Cotton Club: A Pictorial and Social History of the Most Famous Symbol of the Jazz Era.*
Director of Photography: Stephen Goldblatt.
Set decoration: Richard Sylbert.
Original score: John Barry.
Original music: Duke Ellington, Cab Calloway.
Costume design: Milena Canonero.
Choreography: Michael Smuin.
Editing: Barry Malkin and Richard Q. Lovett.
Assistant editor: Gian Carlo Coppola.
Cast: Richard Gere (Dixie Dwyer), Gregory Hines (Sandman Williams), Diane Lane (Vera Cicero), Lonette McKee (Lila Rose Oliver), Bob Hoskins (Owney Madden), James Remar (Dutch Schultz), Nicholas Cage (Vincent Dwyer), Allen Garfield (Abbadabba Berman), Fred Gwynne (Frenchy DeMange), Gwen Verdon (Mrs. Tish Dwyer), Lisa Jane Persky (Frances Flegenheimer), Maurice Hines (Clay Williams), Julian Beck (Sol Weinstein), Larry Fishburne (Bumpy Rhodes), John Ryan (Joe Flynn), Larry Marshall (Cab Calloway), Zane Mark (Duke Ellington), Joe Dallessandro (Lucky Luciano).
Premiere: December 1984 in the United States.